he Second Book of THE ADVENTURES OF  W9-CHP-631 ...HAL

HIRED TO DEFEND

enjoy MARY ANN,

Moocyn

MADELYN I. SAWYER

outskirtspress

DENVER, COLORADO

Outskirts Press, Inc.
http://www.outskirtspress.com

ISBN: 978-1-4787-2696-8

Library of Congress Control Number: 2014902594

PRINTED IN THE UNITED STATES OF AMERICA

For Monica and Mike

Contents

Part I

CHAPTER 1

Pleading For Mercy

"Wait. Wait. Wait," he yelled running full speed down the jet way bridge. From where I was sitting, it appeared he didn't need to get on the airplane because he was already airborne by the time he reached the Delta Air Lines employee that was closing the forward cabin door.

From my first class seat, on the starboard side of the aircraft, I could see directly into the jet way ramp, giving me a clear view of every furrowed line on the distressed man's face as he pleaded with the agent to let him board the aircraft. His thinning hair was a mess, sweat poured down his shiny forehead and dripped onto his tan, tropical suit. He was red-faced, panting loudly, and pleading to be allowed on the aircraft.

Oh, this is going to be good. I thought as the scene in front of me unfolded.

The agent sternly advised the man that he could not board because it was already cleared for departure, the clock was ticking, and he was too late. "Sorry buddy, you missed this one. You need to go back to the gate and speak with the agent. She'll book you on another flight to Haiti." The agent said with firmly while shaking his head.

The man didn't budge and I watched the man and the ticket agent continue to exchange words. I wasn't alarmed, I was curious as to what was going to happen next because I knew the man who was trying desperately to board the aircraft.

As the man continued to plead - whine actually - I saw from the corner of my eye Agent Tony Lopez, our team leader, moving quickly toward to the cabin door. He moved with rapid speed and determination. I could hear his feet pound as he moved down the aisle towards the forward section of the aircraft.

When he reached the door, he began speaking quickly, his Latin accent taking on a strange twist of English and Spanish as he spoke with the ticket agent, hands at his sides, his voice just barely a whisper. I couldn't hear what was being said even though I was just a few seats away, but their body language told me it was getting heated.

In the meantime the agitated man trying to board had become very still, seemingly awaiting his fate, looking as scared as a man facing criminal charges after being arrested. No chance of escape, no chance to run, no more excuses.

As the gate agent and Lopez continued their discussion, the cockpit door creaked open and the first officer said, "We're ready to depart and you two are holding up the show. So what's going on here?"

The lead flight attendant had told him that there was some sort of disturbance going on at the main aircraft door, not a fight, but a discussion that both parties seemed unable to resolve.

"I don't know what's going on," the flight attendant told the first officer. "But for some reason one of the air marshals are involved."

A low murmur buzzed thru the aircraft as heads peeked between the aisles, looking toward the front of the plane. Everyone who could look towards the front did so with curious anticipation. A few bolder, more brazen, and nosy passengers' were now standing with their hands resting on the seat backs in front of them, watching the spectacle unfold.

"Enough!" the exasperated first officer said. "We're leaving, and we're leaving now." In disgust, he pointed at the ground agent to get off the aircraft. In the same breath, he told the man wanting to board to do so immediately. "Get this man a seat, quickly please," he said to the flight attendant hovering nearby saying.

As the newly-boarded man walked through the first class cabin area, he looked down at me, making solid eye contact as he indicated that I should get up and follow the flight attendant because I was in his previously assigned seat. I gave him a hard stare that said, *Go to hell, I'm not moving.*

Yes, Mr. Punctual was one of our very own, and I was sitting comfortably in his first class seat.

Team members are given their seat assignments the day before they are scheduled to fly to assure that each team member dresses according to the class of service they will be sitting in. Thankfully, I was dress appropriately and I was moved to first class because of his apparent "no show" at check-in time.

Not a chance would I even consider changing seats I thought to myself. The early bird gets the worm, as my Grandmother Irene always use to say.

Passing by me as he followed the flight attendant, I heard the pilot say to him, "This isn't the end of this Bucko. Grab a seat so we can get the hell out of here before we lose our clearance." And with that, the first officer disappeared into the cockpit; the cabin door was closed, secured. I swear I could see fumes seeping out from under the cockpit door.

Looking embarrassed, pissed off, stressed, and very sweaty the air marshal took his seat. He knew, I knew, and every other team member onboard knew that he was in a heap of trouble and had potentially jeopardized his fellow team members by his nearly missing the flight.

And now, everyone onboard knew that there were at least two air marshals traveling: Agent Lopez and Agent Morris. The team's pucker factor went up several notches, as if we needed anything else to worry about. *Okay, Maggie.*

It's time to really, really pay attention, girl.

Scan, scan, scan, I knew with full certainty that this flight was no longer secure for our team, and we had no idea if there were any terrorist onboard or not.

I frowned, and thought to myself, *if there are bad guys onboard they wouldn't arrive late and allow themselves to be identified, what a mess.*

Thankfully, after two hours of feeling like everyone's eyes were boring into the back of my head, we landed in Haiti without incident. I had a wallop of a headache. My eyes felt as dry as the Sonora Desert near Marana where we trained, and I was more than ready to stretch, get out of my seat, and go to the bathroom. With everything that happened before we took off, I didn't dare leave my designated zone uncovered on this mission. *Nope, not a chance Maggie, this girl is staying put.*

After all the passengers deplaned, and the ground crew boarded to clean, I heard Agent Lopez call Agent Morris to the back of the aircraft, "What the hell were you thinking Gene?"

"You not only almost missed the flight-well, in reality you should have missed it you moron. You put this entire team in jeopardy, embarrassed the heck out of me in front of the Captain, his entire crew, and all of the passengers!" Agent Lopez yelled.

"What happened?" He demanded.

"I got up late, missed my tee time, so my golf game got started late, and well…you know the rest of the story," Agent Morris said with little apology.

Agent Morris actually looked defiant. It was almost as if he couldn't believe he was being questioned about being late.

Wow, I guess he's a bigger fool than I originally thought.

I knew Morris was an avid golfer. In fact, he had told me on several occasions that he wanted to turn pro when he retired from the Federal Aviation Administration (FAA). He felt he was that good. He was already a golf instructor at a local country club in his hometown-so turning pro to him seemed like the next logical step.

From what I could see and hear, Agent Lopez was going to have a stroke. "What!" he screamed. "No, no, never mind, I don't want to hear anymore. I'll deal with you when we get back to Miami. Go sit down. Get out of my way. And get out of my sight." Agent Lopez screamed.

As for me, I got off the aircraft faster than I ever had before. I bounded down the jet way stairs, two at a time, almost skipping, as I physically and mentally began readying myself to assume my "Caribbean Swag" position at the bottom of the stairs.

I call it the Caribbean Swag because you needed to look tough as hell, ready to take out anyone who so much as stepped within the foot print of the aircraft that wasn't supposed to be there. I was in the open, exposed, as I waited for the arrival of the next plane load of passengers, but I felt as mean and tough as I looked.

Baking in the hot sun was a much better fate than Morris was about to receive. "It's good to be me," I sang to myself.

Flying day trips between Miami and Haiti became grueling after about the seventh day of our ten-day mission. Agent Lopez, from the Miami Security Field Office, and my colleague, Agent Stanton, from the Los Angeles Security Field Office, along with the rest of the team, had sunburned noses, necks, arms, and hands from standing on the viscid black tarmac. As we watched, evaluated, and judged each Delta Air Lines passenger who either walked in to or out of the small airline terminal at the Port A Prince Airport we felt the blistering sun, coupled with the sweltering tarmac showed us no mercy. No mercy in making sure that each team member standing guard was an uncomfortable as they could possibly be.

The two-hour flights to and from Haiti, and the hours of standing guard before and after flying had wore on the team, but the threat was real, the mission necessary, and the flights needed protection. With that being the case, we carried on with our Caribbean Swag attitudes, by looking as mean as possible each and every second that we were in public view.

I've got this, piece of cake, I chanted to myself while feeling the sweat drip down the back of my shirt. It was barely stopped by the belt that held my firearm holster firmly in place. But my holster was empty because my firearm was visible, solidly gripped in my left hand, barrel pointing safely towards the ground. My index finger rested softly against the metal trigger guard. My hand was as stable as a slab of Yosemite granite as I held the rubber grip of my gun. I was ready to fire at the first sign of a threat.

After this morning's mishap with Morris, I could sense that our team was not in their usual upbeat moods: we were tired and on edge.

Our Federal Air Marshal (FAM) team had been assembled quickly for this assignment; even my supervisor, Rob Drake, back in Los Angeles had expressed his surprise when he received the call to deploy me and Agent Stanton immediately to Miami for a mission with just a few days' notice. I remember just last week him hollering from across the room, "Get ready to pack your bags again, you two. You're off to Miami for another air marshal mission." And here we were, quickly assembled, but it made sense now-with the rising political unrest in Haiti the FAA had been requested to deploy federal air marshal teams on all U.S. aircraft flying in and out of Haiti until its government stabilized and the threat of hijacking subsided.

As Agent Lopez had described a few days earlier, the tactics were completely different than how we had been trained. We were trained to be a covert cadre, displaying our firearms only when the threat presented itself. But here, in these circumstances, our team was told that the threat was already visible in that people wanted more than anything to escape this island. Our team needed to be visible to thwart any attempt to board the flights that were carrying people away from this impoverished place. Especially, under no circumstances, was anyone allowed inside the aircraft that was not authorized onboard.

The days were long and exhausting. Combined with the exposure to the elements and the passenger visibility this entire mission was filled with fatigue. And there wasn't any time to get in a short run or work out which always helped me deal with exhaustion.

In these conditions we had to be careful to watch one another's back and not snap. When the last passenger had boarded, the flight attendant nodded down to us, her squinted eyes and hand motions, indicating that it was time for us to board the aircraft. Agent Stanton and I quickly holstered our firearms and ran up the silver metal stairs two at a time, stopping just short of entering the aircraft to scan the ramp, terminal, and fence line filled with people who were watching our every move. As each of us passed by the flight attendant, we glanced to our left to see that the cockpit door had been secured, meaning the flight was just about ready, and we needed to be seated quickly. I was in the forward section of the aircraft and Agent Stanton was aft. Once we were seated, you could hear the ground air- conditioning unit disconnect and we could immediately feel the cabin temperature begin to warm up as the hot, Caribbean air seeped inside the aircraft. The cabin took on a musty, sweaty smell, as fans were pulled out of pockets, purses, and invisible places inside Caribbean dresses as passengers rapidly fanned themselves in a futile attempt to ward off the rising temperature. It was indeed time to get airborne, at least then we could cool off.

Buckled in, watching, waiting, listening, I thought, *three years into this Maggie, four years in a couple of months, and gosh do I love this job!* A smile crept into the corners of my mouth and the tiny crow's feet that were beginning to form around the outer corners of my eyes crinkled.

I was already officially off my one-year probationary period now so the government Standard Form, SF-50 that I found on my desk last week brought a smile to my lips. Sitting in the yellow "For my eyes only" envelope was the notification that I had been converted from a "career conditional" employee to a "career" employee. This milestone of federal employment added additional benefits and protection and I was well on my way with my career as a federal agent.

The other two seat mates in my row never so much as looked at me. They both pretended to be reading, but their magazine pages never turned. They sat very still and silent as if they had been turned to stone. Once again, the Caribbean Swag worked, at least, in this row.

"Ah, another *quiet flight Maggie,"* I thought.

CHAPTER 2

What A Chump

While sitting on this hot, smelly aircraft, waiting to taxi and take-off, I reflected back on the crash of Pacific Southwest Airlines flight 1771 in California, in December 1987. A tragic crash created by a disgruntled airline employee that began my career as a federal air marshal.

Within a year of being hired, I somberly watched again on television, in 1988, Pan American Airline's flight 103 lying in ruins in Scotland. Both tragedies were created by acts of terrorism: the first an insider threat caused by an airline employee, and the second by terrorists whose only desire was to kill Americans. Both events created a massive hiring of federal air marshals and special agents within the Department of Transportation's Federal Aviation Administration.

Every air marshal trainee went through extensive training in the high desert near Marana, Arizona. To qualify, we logged hundreds of hours running, working out in the gym, and going through tactical training on mock aircraft, coupled with hours on the pistol range. We trained at night, during the day, in the blistering heat of the summer, or frigid temperatures of the winter, to qualify. Our air marshal qualifications standards where higher than any other federal agency including the world-famous FBI. Then year after year, we found our way back to this desert training facility to re-qualify. We were hired to protect, hired to defend, hired to serve this great country of ours.

My nickname was "Mad Dog," a name given me during an early morning training run during my fourth week of basic training. Every single day I ran, always trying to imagine that I was chasing bad guys, chasing evil before it could chase me down, I had managed to outrun everyone in my class, shouting along the way as if I was a mad woman. I gave it my all – and Mad Dog – emerged that day like a hungry coyote emerging from the desert floor looking for food, and knowing that she might have to fight to keep it. Since that day, Mad Dog hasn't left me; now I'm even more confident, fit, cocky, and aware of my surroundings.

Once again, I was in another part of the world, protecting airline passengers from a different type of threat, but a threat none-the-less. The political situation in Haiti had greatly declined since 1986, the country was poorer than ever, the politics were corrupt, and citizens were looking for a quick escape from their homeland. A ride on a United States commercial aircraft seemed like a logical solution for many.

As we lifted off, the aircraft was still stifling hot. You could smell the perspiration of the sweaty passengers, and you could sense their relief as well. We were finally airborne. And in a few short hours we'd land in Miami where another world and lifestyle awaited them. *Yes indeed, we are blessed to live in America* is all I could think of as we bumped along, lifting up and away from the tiny island rich with poverty and despair.

The lady next to me was as black as I've ever seen. Her skin was pulled tight across her plump, round face and it was perfectly smooth. There wasn't a wrinkle or tiny line anywhere. I was not only amazed at her smooth skin, I was jealous. I was jealous because tiny wrinkles were beginning to form across my forehead, checks, and around my eyes.

Her eyes were half shut, her hands gripping the arm rests, as she waited for the turbulence to subside so she could continue reading the book she had sitting on her lap. Her lips moved ever so slightly, as if in silent prayer, waiting patiently, knowing the Lord would take care of her. I myself, found solace and beauty in her faith.

I believed in God, thanking the Lord first thing in the morning as my eyes slowly opened before getting out of bed. Today, my faith was two-fold, my faith in God, as strong and powerful as ever, and my faith in my concealed firearm tucked beneath my light weight jacket. My continual faith, believing in the team I was traveling with, for all of us would become a line of defense against anyone who wanted to cause us harm.

I was seated closest to the cockpit for this leg of our mission. If I was any closer I'd be sitting in the forward lavatory. I fully knew the importance of my strategic seat assignment.

"Protect the cockpit, at all cost," Agent Lopez had instructed me to do in Miami before we started the first leg of this flight. "Remember to always scan, listen, watch, and act if someone gets anywhere near that cockpit door. You're the one Maggie. We're counting on you to maintain control of your zone. He stated with a serious voice. I nodded my head in the affirmative, letting him know that I completely understood my responsibilities and that I would maintain the integrity of my zone.

Once we leveled off, escaping the warm winds that lifted us away from Haiti, the lady next to me uncurled her clenched, sweaty fingers, letting go of the airplane arm rests, as she visibly began relaxing. I heard her say, "Thank you Jesus." Under her breath as she touched her book in preparation to begin reading.

I briefly looked at her, but she still refused to make eye contact with me. Can't say I didn't blame her, but I still had to look. *Maggie, Maggie, you really are nice, it's just sometimes people can't see your charm.*

The magazine I brought with me was about running. I started thumbing through it, while watching and listening to the aircraft's sound. So far, so good- quiet-except for the air vents above our heads, gushing air into the cabin in a vain attempt to cool us off. I heard a baby crying several seats behind me and a Mother's calm voice trying to lull her baby into silence with coos and whispers of love-so far it wasn't working.

The flight attendants rattled drink and snack carts as they began their preparation to appease the passengers on this short two-hour flight. As they busily prepared their carts, I silently commended them as they place one of the food service carts between the cockpit and the rest of the cabin. This positioning provided another layer of protection, making it more difficult for a terrorist to access the cockpit.

This flight team looked young, but that move, positioning the cart in front of the cockpit door, told me they had listened to our briefings earlier in the day and that they were eager to assist us in any way they could, in keeping this aircraft and her passengers safe. It was a good feeling that we were all working as a team.

The flight attendants began serving each passenger with a drink of their choice and a few bags of peanuts. The flight was too short for a meal service, so the peanuts were handed out with a generous hand. From the beginning of the service to the end it took about forty-five minutes. By the time the carts were stowed, we were within thirty minutes of landing in Miami.

The landing was much smoother than the one we had endured earlier. Miami was flat which prevented the updrafts that we experienced flying in and out of Haiti. There was a smattering of applause as many of the passengers welcomed the ground after landing.

Our seatbelts were barley unbuckled before the excited passengers were out of their seats, pulling down luggage from the overhead bins and jostling for their position to escape this aircraft. The cabin began to warm up again as the power was shut-down and the air conditioning truck had not yet arrived.

I eased my way forward and stood with my back to the cockpit door in the "military rest" position with my feet slightly positioned apart, arms at my sides, and my eyes scanning the cabin, looking for trouble, looking for anything that appeared to be out-of-place.

Okay Maggie, keep watching everyone, keep listening, and wait, while everyone gets off the aircraft. This has been one heck of a day, so don't let your guard down now.

As I looked into the cabin and over the tops of the seats, I could barely see Agent Stanton standing. He too was waiting for the passengers in his zone to leave the aircraft. He glanced forward and we briefly made eye contact, silently signaling that everything was okay. It had been a long day, and I knew our team was as anxious to finish up this trip. We silently waited until each passenger left the aircraft before we conducted a quick sweep to ensure nothing dangerous was left onboard. Then we allowed the cleaning crew to board so they could get the aircraft ready for the next group of passengers.

I wasn't sure where this aircraft was going next, but I knew the flights to and from Haiti were finished for the day. We, like the flight crew, were wrapping up the logistics of our day and would soon be heading to the hotel. Without any doubt, I was ready for a swim, a meal, and a very full glass of white wine.

We rode to the hotel in complete silence. Agent Lopez was still stinging from the rotten day and a compromised mission by one of our own. Everyone else on the team followed suit by keeping quiet.

Just inside the hotel lobby, Lopez barked, "Meet in room 317 in fifteen minutes. And don't any of you dare be late." With that comment he pushed the elevator door button and disappearing into the elevator without offering or allowing anyone to ride along with him.

"Ha, glad I didn't get in that elevator with him." I said to Agent Stanton.

"Yep, me too, see you in fifteen – I'm taking the stairs."

"Wait up, I'll race you! This meeting might take awhile so this might be my only exercise for the day."

When I got to my room on the seventh floor I was winded, but I was so wound up, I probably could have raced to the fifteenth floor without a thought.

I didn't even bother to change. I quickly washed my face, feeling the cool, fresh water streak across my skin in big splashes. I combed my long blonde hair, pulling it back into a pony tail. I didn't have any makeup on, so I didn't need to touch that up, but I did want to brush my teeth and collect my thoughts before heading down to room 317.

Finishing up in the bathroom, I had a couple of minutes to spare so I gazed out the window at the view I had of the roof covering the hotel lobby, complete with heating-and-air conditioning units. Sadly, I couldn't see any of the aircraft movement around the Miami International Airport (MIA) that the hotel was located on. Pity, I love airplanes and their graceful movement between the boundaries of earth.

I looked at my watch and decided I better get back downstairs. I wasn't going to make it my time to be late.

The door to room 317 was propped open with a tennis shoe; I could hear voices all at once, so I knew the meeting hadn't started. *Thank goodness, I'm on time* I thought to myself as I pushed the door open and walked into a room full of marshals, doing what they do best – telling tall stories and bigger lies!

"Hi," I said to Agent Stanton as I plopped down on one of the double beds.

"Hi kiddo, hell of a day, wasn't it?"

"That's an understatement. I can't wait to hear this debrief." I said with a sly grin.

"Me either, but I think we're all going to catch hell for this flight, not just Morris over there." A team's a team, and we've got to stick together, so we're all in trouble I suspect."

I shrugged, Great, I just love teamwork."

The door swung open abruptly as Agent Lopez appeared, pushing a silver serving cart. "Hold that door," he commanded of anyone that was nearest to the now swinging door.

Lopez rolled the cart over to the window and stopped the cart between the TV and the bed closest to the window. The cart was full of snacks, beer, and a bottle of chardonnay. Several of us looked around at one another with questioning looks.

"I know this looks like a party, but it's not," began Lopez. "It's been one hell of a day, I'm tired, I'm especially thirsty, but we've got some important things to discuss that can't be discussed in the lounge downstairs. So I decided to bring the lounge to us. Grab some snacks and a beverage of choice. Let's start shall we?"

I poured myself a glass of wine and sat down on the floor with my back propped against the wall between the front door and the closet. It felt great to stretch my legs out flat on the floor and have a little space between me and my fellow marshals. Lopez's hotel room was full to capacity and stuffy. But it was private, so the heated discussion that was about to commence was primed and ready to begin.

"The first thing I'm going to say is that this will never *happen* again. I do not want to have our team jeopardized the way it was today because one of you decided to make your personal life a priority when you are on government time." Lopez sternly said.

"When you leave your house to go on a mission, you are on the clock 24/7, even if you're not flying. It's just how it is," he continued.

"And being late because you missed your tee time won't fly with me," Lopez said as he looked directly at Morris, his eyes ablaze. "Now, I want to hear your story again Morris."

Red faced, Morris told his tale to the group just as he told Lopez. He did it with no apology as he finished off his beer and began chewing on the potato chips he had taken from the cart. As he finished, dribbles of chip crumbs dotted his navy blue golf shirt like tiny dabs of dandruff.

What a chump, I thought to myself. He doesn't even give a shit, except he's embarrassed and he knows he'll be written up for being late.

When an employee in the federal government gets written up it means, potentially, that you won't receive a favorable performance appraisal at the end of the year. When that happens, you won't receive a pay increase the following year. And down the road, it impacts your retirement pension.

Tough, but *he deserves everything he gets,* I thought.

After another hour of discussion, Lopez cut us all loose for the evening.

"Okay, everybody scram. I'll see all of you in the lobby at 0500 hours and don't even think about being late. In fact, if you are, just pack your bags and go home."

We stacked our empty glasses and cans on the serving cart as we scooted past it, quickly disappearing into the empty and very musty hallway.

It's time to disappear girly-girl, I thought as I headed for the exit door. I was planning on taking the stairs as fast as I could to escape the sense of frustration that was engulfing the team.

When I got back upstairs to my room, looking at my watch I knew it was too late to go for a run and way too early to go to bed. I didn't feel like talking much after our almost two-hour meeting either.

"And without any doubt, I'm done looking at anyone for the day." I said out loud as I looked in the mirror that was bolted to the wall in my room.

Still hungry, I ordered room service, one more glass of wine, while deciding to write a few more post cards to my family and my significant other, Dave.

Dave was a dreamy airline pilot, flying for a cargo company that was based in Dallas, Texas. He flew a lot into Florida and down into the Caribbean so we didn't see each other a lot, but he had come to California to visit and I traveled to visit him in Texas. We even met in Las Vegas and New Mexico a few times to make a fun weekend out of our times together.

I hadn't planned on getting into a long distance relationship, much less getting serious since my last serious relationship was a total disaster. The disaster being - yes, the distance hurt, but that wasn't it - I found out he was married. That was the kiss of death. I found out when his wife called me while I was in basic training to become an air marshal. Unbelievable, I was crushed, mortified, and mad all at the same time. I swore I'd never trust a man again, but somehow time allowed the bad taste to fade, and then I met Dave.

Dave was smart, funny, good looking, thin and didn't mind spending money on you. He wasn't as athletic as I was, in fact pulling the handle on slot machines and doing odds and ends around the house was his definition of exercise, but he was in pretty good shape, and we had a lot of things in common. In just a few months of our relationship blossoming, I was pretty sure I was falling in love with the guy.

"I know, I know Maggie, this may be a disaster in the works, but I gotta say I like this guy a lot," I hummed excitedly as I scribbled my hellos on Dave's postcard.

We both loved adventure, travel, we loved airplanes, and we respected one another's career. We hadn't figured out our living arrangements yet, I was still based in California and Dave was in Dallas, but I had recently submitted a transfer request to the Dallas/Fort Worth CASFO.

I knew the office had received my package because I heard through the grapevine that the supervisor in Dallas had called my supervisor. I also heard that Supervisor Drake didn't want to lose me, but he understood my desire to move to Texas to be with my significant other.

Yep, Maggie, I am one lucky lady. Our phone bills are outrageous! I laughed. *Sure glad I get paid lots of over time when I'm flying.*

Dave and I sent postcards from wherever we were, saying the usual "Wish you were here" sentence, along with fond wishes for safe trips, and hopes to "See you soon". It was fun and exciting to see a postcard in your mailbox from the one you loved.

This postcard was no different. I had bought one in the gift shop downstairs; it had the Miami skyline and the Atlantic Ocean glistening in the background. It was just a plain, pretty much no-distinct card, but I enjoyed writing a quick note to say hello and to tell him that I had some fun stories to tell about this "vacation", as I called it, when I saw him next.

I licked the stamp, put a kiss on the postcard, lipstick that I never wore, but had acquired for this very thing-my personal post mark, much more enticing than the dull U.S. postage stamp beside it. Just as I finished up, a light rap at the door came with a call of "room service" from a female voice on the other side of the door.

"Good evening Miss" the server said as I opened the door. "Where would you like me to put your dinner?"

"Put in on the little table there by the window, please. That would be great, thanks."

With a nod of her head, she walked across the room and put the tray down. My glass of wine had plastic wrap across the top and it lightly swayed in the glass as she set the tray on the table.

I signed the room service tab she handed to me and gave her a tip, the tab, and her pen.

"Thank you very much," said the polite young woman. "Enjoy your evening."

"I will, you too." I said and I closed the door quietly.

I ate my Caesar salad and garlic bread, and sipped on my glass of wine while channel flipping. It was getting late. The evening news was over hours ago, and most of the channels showed shows that I either knew nothing about or didn't want to see. So as soon as I finished eating I turned off the TV, put my dishes back onto the serving tray and placed the tray on the floor outside of my room door so the night service could come collect them.

I decided to take a long shower, read some, and call it a night. It had been a long grueling day, but the end was in sight. In fact, this mission would be over in a couple of days, and I'd be back at home in Redondo Beach loving life.

"I'm never late, but I definitely don't plan on being late tomorrow, or ever, after witnessing what happened today," I whispered to myself as I set my alarm for 0400 hours and opened my book to read for a while.

The next morning I was in the lobby fifteen minutes early to make absolutely sure that I was not late. I dropped my postcard to Dave off in the mailbox that was located next to the front desk and walked over to the chairs in the main lobby area to wait. I had poured a cup of coffee from the coffee machine in the room and brought it downstairs with me.

It was weak, dreadful tasting coffee, but with it being dark outside still, I psychologically felt better having the awful, tepid cup in my hand.

"Why is hotel room coffee always so terrible?" I said when I walked to Agent Stanton. "It's bitter and weak as heck."

"Well, good morning to you too." He said with his rough and gruff John Wayne voice. "I see your enjoying your morning cup."

"Yes I am." I laughed. "I've just got to have coffee in the morning, no matter how bad it is."

During the next fifteen minutes, Lopez and the rest of the team arrived with various expressions of wear and tear. The trip wasn't particularly long, only ten days, but the ground conditions, short turn rounds, and extreme weather conditions was beginning to pull all of the energy from this team. By looking around at each member's face I could tell everyone was ready for this mission to be over.

"Just one more day, Kiddo. We're about done with this one." Agent Stanton said to me. "Come on let's get to the airport and find a real cup of coffee."

"I'm for that."

We climbed into the airport shuttle silently taking our seats, staring once again out the windows on our short ride to the airport's main terminal area. Since it was so early we were the only ones on the bus, so we all sat in separate rows, stretching out, relaxing, and watching the sky change colors from its deep dark black to pale shades of gray alerting the world that daylight is coming.

As I looked out the window, enjoying the sunrise, I looked forward to finding a good cup of coffee.

I love airports. I love airplanes. Ever since I was a little kid my chin always tilted upward at the sound of a turbine engine racing by or when seeing a jet streaking through the sky. Jet fuel was in my veins, it had to be, because I could feel the tug of the world map, beckoning me to distant lands as I twirled the world globe. Come *see me, come and fly to my country,* each little colored country on the globe chanted.

Airports are magical because they transport people to and from places far and near. Some people travel for business, others for pleasure.

I love watching people's faces some filled with excitement, tension, or joy. Some type of emotion is always visible, clearly painted on their faces.

Airports are cities unto themselves. They temporarily house families, assist people when they get lost or sick, fight crime, and find heroes to call their own.

Today, Miami International Airport was just as magical as any other day. Travelers were being dropped off curb-side by loved ones, taxis, or shuttle vans to begin their travel adventures. It was interesting to see everyone tugging and toting bags along as they made their way to the ticket counters in anticipation of the day ahead.

Our team walked through the terminal to the Delta Air Lines ticket counter and signaled one of the supervisors that we had arrived and needed to check-in for our flight.

As the team began gathering and waiting in various locations around the ticket area, Agent Stanton and I quickly grabbed cups of coffee from the newspaper stand that was just a few feet away from the end of the long airline counter. As I sipped my first cup of real coffee, you could hear me sigh-a sigh full of pure contentment. I was now truly ready to face the day.

Agent Lopez signaled the team to follow him as an airline supervisor began leading the team back behind the ticket counter to board our flight. This seemed a bit obvious, especially if anyone was paying attention to our gathering at the end of the ticket counter, but each airline had established their preferred way to board marshals. It was either proceeding behind the ticket counter or go through the security checkpoint. Both options had it pluses and minuses.

"Off we go to face the day." I said as I held my coffee cup up to salute the new day.

"Yep, one more day of flying, then we can pack and head for home. I can say I'm ready and so is Roberta. She's always holding down the fort, kids and a full-time butt kicker of a job. She and I have plans this weekend: I'm taking her out for a romantic dinner. And, I'm ready to see my kids." Agent Stanton said.

"Dave's trip schedule is sending him out today, so I bet it will be a few more weeks before we see each other. Juggling our lives is a lot of work!" I sighed.

"Long distance relationships – you know you're going to have to do something about that someday, Maggie." Then Stanton went on to say, "Roberta and I commuted for a few years when we first met. But she finally gave in and moved from San Diego to L.A. to be with me."

"I didn't know that," I said. "Leaving San Diego must have been hard, but you're worth it, I bet." I said and I punched him in the arm.

With that, Agent Stanton beamed and said, "Hell yaw, I'm worth it!"

"Let's board," Lopez said. "Let's get to work."

CHAPTER 3

Flying High

A thousand miles away in Dallas, Texas, Captain Dave was getting ready to fly. First Officer Todd was out doing a pre-flight check of their C-131 aircraft by walking around and inspecting her. Dave was in the flight operations office gathering up the flight plans, along with weather information.

Today's cargo payload would take him from Dallas to Miami and into Puerto Rico for their overnight. The following day, they'd reverse the route back to Dallas. He knew his flight path would be criss-crossing the skies close to where his Maggie was flying, but unfortunately they had no way of connecting or talking to one another.

Dave collected the rest of his flight planning paperwork, picked up his black flight bag full of Jepson charts, thanked the dispatcher, and walked towards his plane. He whistled under his breath, pulling air between his teeth, as he trekked along the ramp.

"Sure do miss that girl," he muttered to himself. "Didn't think I would so much, but I do."

Outside, he gazed at the morning sky, full of reds, grays, and blues, studied the wind sock lightly fluttering in the wind and he knew that this day was going to be a splendid day for flying. As the sailor's adage goes, red skies in the morning sailors delight. Pilots love red skies in the morning too, a sign usually indicating that it would be a smooth day for flying.

Dallas-Love Field (DAL) was a great airport with nice long runway, which was a great comfort for cargo pilots who flew heavy payloads for a living.

Once the walk-around preflight was complete Captain Dave and First Officer Todd got busy with their cockpit preflight checklist. One more set of standard instructions to abide by to make sure every flight procedure was followed before they taxied out for take-off. In the world of aviation, it is imperative to have layers and layers of safety checks so when and if anything goes wrong the pilots have half a chance to get the aircraft down safely and out alive.

"Checklist complete," Todd said in a firm, loud voice.

"Roger that, call the tower for taxi instructions so we can get this bird out of here and get some work done."

As they taxied down the runway they both watched the instrument panel in front of them, constantly looking out the front and side cockpit windows for any other aircraft, ground equipment, or even birds that might cause them trouble on their way to their departure runway. Everything was in order and soon they were in position and cleared for take-off.

"Antilles 23, taxi into position and hold 27 left," said the calming voice of the air traffic controller.

"Wilco, we'll taxi into position and hold on runway 27 left," First Officer Todd advised the tower.

Once in position both pilots scanned their surrounding once again and waited for clearance instructions from the air traffic control tower.

"Antilles 23, winds 240 at 5, you are cleared to take-off Runway 27 left."

"Roger that, cleared for take-off 27 left. Thank you ATC, good day." First Officer Todd said. "Here we go Captain" First Officer Todd said and with that they began their departure sequence. As they rolled down the runway, First Officer Todd called out V-1, then V-2 and Captain Dave pulled up on the throttle, and they gently lifted off the ground, as smoothly as the cushion of air they were floating upon. Further into the sequence they pulled up their landing gear and began their three-hour flight to Miami.

Once again, Newton's Third Law of Motion didn't let them down. That law being: along with every action there is an equal and opposite reaction. 'Lift' had once again gently carried them airborne and the aircraft settled out at their assigned flight level, moving across the state of Texas, Louisiana, and Georgia, as they flew south towards Florida.

After landing in Miami they taxied to the cargo ramp near their company's hangar to have their cargo off-loaded and new cargo loaded for their flight to Puerto Rico. It was a long day, sometimes a bit boring, but the pay and company benefits were good, and the flight schedule was well organized for plenty of time off.

"We've got a couple hours here so I'm going to call Maggie," Dave said.

"Fine by me because I better call my wife and see how she's doing." Todd said in reply.

The afternoon sun was already heating up the company office when Dave walked in. The enormous windows allowed lot of sunshine to spill into the office along with a full view of the cargo ramp. The floors were worn and dingy, stating the obvious that no one cared about them. The scuffed floors, full of black marks and dirt definitely showed their wear and tear. Not a single passenger would ever see these dirty, tired floors, only cargo agents moving paper back and forth; while watching out those big windows as boxes, an occasional coffin, or animals were loaded onboard for their flight either to Puerto Rico or Dallas, about the only two destinations these birds flew.

Leaning of the edge of the desk piled high with cargo manifests, picking up the phone, Dave dialed Maggie's home number. It was 4 P.M. in California by now, so there was an off chance that she'd be home. "I miss my girl."

"Hello."

"Hi Maggie, my gorgeous woman, this is your Captain David. How are you Missy?"

"Hi Honey, I'm really, really good. I just walked in the door; man-oh-man this mission was crazy. There was more drama from our team than from any terrorist that's for sure. You'll love the story when I tell you." I said almost in one breath. "How are you? Where are you? I miss you."

"I miss you too! Sweetie, I can't wait to see you. I'll be home in a few days. I'm in Miami and on my way to Puerto Rico. Overnight there and head back, direct, to Dallas tomorrow."

"Good. After this mission, I'm back in the office for about a month I think, so we'll all have time together either in Dallas or here. If you come here, maybe we could go to Catalina and take a mini-vacation." I said with a smile on my face.

"We'll definitely have time together when I get back from this trip. It's time to catch-up." Dave said.

"Okay, it's a date honey. Who are you flying with?"

"I'm crewing with First Officer Todd. You haven't met him yet. He's a good guy; originally from Finland, but he's been in the states about ten years."

"And speaking of Todd, he just walked in the door which means it's probably time to get going. I miss you Maggie, and I'll see you soon. Okay?" Dave said in a quiet and tender voice.

"I miss you too sweetie. I can't wait to see you. Call when you get home. I'll be thinking about you. Big, big hugs and kisses from me."

With reluctance we both hung up. "Distance does make the heart grow fonder," I quietly said.

Dave was ten years older than me, divorced, with a son. His ex and their son lived in Michigan. I'd never dated an older man; especially divorced with a son, but somehow we clicked.

We met on a flight from Los Angeles to Dallas about eight months ago. I was already settled in my seat and the door was about to close, so I was silently hoping that the middle seat next to me would remain empty so I could have more room. Little did I know that having that seat occupied was going to change, and rock, my world. As we lifted off, we immediately hit it off, talking the entire flight. We've have been talking and seeing each other ever since.

After talking with Dave I was all pent up inside and needed to get the wiggles out of me. I needed to get outside. I was still training to run my first marathon, but for now just a few miles would be enough. I was tired, but I knew I'd sleep better if I went for a run, plus I needed food. I was low on supplies and my refrigerator was as empty and lonely as I felt right now, sitting in my kitchen. I knew I needed to run.

I put on my running shoes, laced them up and began organizing my thoughts. I needed my credit card, a grocery list, and a light jacket. The sun was beginning to fade over Santa Monica Bay so it would be cooling off. I quickly wrote my list, grabbed money from my wallet, house keys, and flew out the door. I took off running north along the Esplanade at a solid, steady, happy pace. At the one mile point, I turned around and headed for the grocery store. I was beginning to feel in sync with the world again, balanced, and at peace. It's amazing what a couple of miles of pounding the payment will do for one's mind, body, and soul.

I love running. I love it because it is a challenging sport, but a sport you can do independently or with other runners. You can take your running shoes anywhere in the world and you'll always have a place to run: inside, outside, stairwells, you name it. I love running because I have to pass a physical fitness test every six months to keep my job too – so running is without a doubt my favorite sport.

After shopping, carrying my bag of groceries, I headed for home at a brisk power walk pace. It was time for a nice glass of Pinot Noir, a salad, and some fresh baked salmon with dill and lemon. I was ready for a home cooked meal!

Kicking off my running shoes, putting on my dilapidated, worn flip-flops, I poured myself a glass of wine and began cooking dinner. I thought about Dave, wishing he was here, sipping wine with me, cooking dinner, and talking about our day, but alas, by now he was en-route to Puerto Rico.

Meanwhile, on final approach into the Luis Munoz Marin International Airport, in Puerto Rico, Captain Dave was beginning his descent for landing. The landing was a little rougher than normal due to the crosswinds buffeting the aircraft. Captain Dave was very experienced with crosswinds' and with skill and the calmness of a cucumber; he slightly crabbed the aircraft to the port-side to counter the crosswind as he eased the plane onto the runway. Only one slight thud was heard as the main gear tires absorbed the landing.

"Well done." Todd said.

"Any landing is a good landing," Dave said with a chuckle. "Hope we didn't burn too much rubber. Don't want to lose my bonus check to new tires this year!"

"Let's get this aircraft taxied to the hangar so we can get the heck out of here. I'm ready for a beer. It's been a long day."

Todd nodded in agreement as they continued to follow the air traffic instructions for taxing to their parking spot on the cargo ramp.

Once the aircraft was safely parked, agriculture was cleared, and the manifest paperwork was given to the contractor Dave and Todd left for the hotel. The contractors would "button up" the aircraft once it was unloaded, and reload her in the morning before Dave and Todd returned for the return flight back to Dallas.

Since this wasn't the main airport terminal, taxi service- or any other type of transportation-was not available, so getting to and from the airport had been difficult until Captain Dave had come up with a solution a few months back.

After almost a year of trying to beg or borrow a ride to the hotel and back, Dave finally bought a beat up car, fondly called "airporter car", which was used by each crew member that needed a ride to their hotel. It was called an "airporter car" because it was dilapidated enough that it could probably only make it to and from the airport. The keys were kept in a lockbox in the contract cargo office and the combination lock afforded some protection that the car would not be stolen. The only condition asked of the other pilots is that the car be kept clean and always had a full tank of gas. It was the pilots ride if these two conditions were met, if not, don't plan on ever asking to use the car again. So far everyone had honored these two simple requests. I think everyone realized pretty quickly how easy Dave had made everyone's trips in Puerto Rico.

The San Juan Resort and Casino was where the crew stayed. It was by far one of the nicest hotels on the island. It was very close to the airport in the city of Carolina, just off Highway 26. This marvelous hotel faced the Atlantic Ocean and close by was the San Jose Laguna. So there were plenty of ocean breezes and views fit for the kings and queens that most airline pilots and crews thought they were. Swimming pools with waterfalls, swim-up bars, and a casino were the final touches that made this an exceptional hotel to stay at.

The only downside to this island paradise was the abundance of hookers that greeted you at every turn inside the main lobby and casino of the hotel. The access to the guest's room was protected by staffed guards at each of the elevator banks, so some security was afforded that you wouldn't have to listen to your neighbors all night.

Theft outside the hotel was also a concern, so if you ventured away from the hotel it paid to be careful.

"Let's get to the hotel guys, daylights' burning," Dave called out to Todd and two other pilots who had just arrived from another flight. "I'm hungry, and I want to play some cards, boys."

As the four men piled into the powder blue four-door Honda civic you could hear the car groan. "I hope the metal frame of this Caribbean rust bucket holds. The price was right so we'll see." Dave said as he buckled his seat-belt.

When the Honda approached rumbling, rattling, and finally stopping in front of him, the valet attendant looking a bit distained as he opened the door for Captain Dave.

"I know, I know, I'm not a Mercedes or a Jaguar, but take good care of my car amigo. I'll need her again in the morning" Dave said as he slipped the attendant a five dollar bill.

Grabbing their flight bags from the musty trunk, their hats off the filthy seats, the four pilots strutted into the hotel to check-in.

The hotel was so frequented by airline personnel that a special check-in counter had been created for flight crews. This hotel was always brimming at the seams with guests: honeymooners, business tycoons, gamblers, and locals that came to gamble. It was a beautiful hotel with lush tropical plants adorning the lobby, and expensive rattan furniture, pottery, and large windows that brought in the light.

Everyone agreed to meet in the lobby lounge for dinner drinks and light snacks before venturing off to gamble or find a more substantial meal.

"See you in about fifteen minutes," Todd said, "I'll drop my bag, wash my face, and I'll be good to go."

"Sounds good."

Fifteen minutes later, comfortably seated in the lobby, everyone had gathered for cocktails. The cute server handed out beers with a welcome smile and a sparkle in her eye.

The pilot talk began and soon the conversation turned from today's flights to stories with a bit more edge to them.

"Did I ever tell you the story when I landed here a few years back in a Caribou and the landing gear collapsed on landing?" Dave asked the pilots.

"No, I've never heard that one." Todd said.

And so the storytelling began. From failed main landing gear, to stalled aircraft, to extreme and terrifying weather. The words flowed, the beer flowed, and the tips flowed to the cute server as if they were rich men and not airline pilots!

It was well after midnight when the pilots ran out of stories. They decided to get some sleep for tomorrow was another day of flying and another chance to rack up some more stories to be told.

CHAPTER 4

Hand Cuffs

Squawking loudly on Monday morning at 5:00 A.M., my Sandhill Crane alarm went off letting me know Monday morning had come at lightning speed and it was already time for me to go to work. I hit the snooze button once in hopes it would forget to wake me up, but alas, it went off again in just a few minutes. I think the second round of my squawking bird alarm was worse than the first time, so I rolled over, said good morning to the Lord, dropped my feet to the floor in search of my flip-flops, and grabbed my robe. Yawning open mouth, I faced another beautiful California-beach morning.

Just over a year and a half ago, I found a little cottage apartment with a garage just a block from the beach. It was like a dream come true; it was adorable and I loved how easy it was to get to the beach every day-well at least every day that I was home.

I had two great neighbors. *No worries about remembering their names, huh Maggie.* I would always laugh to myself. They both had the same name!

Bill and Bill lived in the two apartments above the garages in back of my place. They had ocean views but their apartments were original decor, making them dated. Mine had been completely re-modeled and I was the first tenant to enjoy the beauty of this tiny beach cottage. Everyone had their own one-car garage which was akin to having gold in a beach community where parking was always sparse. The unit next to me had recently been rented after an extensive remodel and the gal that moved in was really, really cool. She worked for a sport network, traveled a lot, but laughed and partied a lot when she was home.

It was wonderful to have great neighbors. I felt like I had found a secret treasure in the midst of a big city. Close to the beach, work, and shopping: a dream location, a dream life, a dream job, and a dreamy guy. I was a happy woman.

"But your boss isn't going to be happy if you don't get a move on Maggie. You lazy girl, get a move on now," I said.

Quickly walking into the tiny kitchen, I turned on the coffee pot, my number one priority as I began getting ready for work. Once I was dressed and re-packed my briefcase, I poured my second cup of coffee, to go this time, and headed out the door. I never gave myself much time to get to work, so I hoped I'd make it on time.

Arriving at the office at ten minutes to six, the parking lot was almost full. I saw Big Earl and another agent heading towards the office building.

Once inside, Agent Stanton was there, of course, he always gets to the office before everyone else. When he saw me, he walked over and gave me a pat on the back.

"Good morning," Stanton said with a grin. "How'd your weekend go?"

"Perfect. How was your weekend?" I said with a smile.

"Good. Coffee?" he said.

"Yep, I'm ready for a refill." And off we headed towards the breakroom with mugs in hand.

The morning passed with a flurry of collecting receipts for my travel voucher and sorting through enforcement cases, and reports that were either potential or already opened violations against air carriers or airport operators. Each case had already been identified with an EIR number, or Enforcement Investigation Report. The report has identification numbers and letters indicating which office opened the case, plus the year and the sequential order number. Identifying a potential violation was determined by measuring the required regulations against the practices or procedures of the party responsible for adhering to the regulation, so for the most part, this was pretty straightforward work. But it was work that always got behind when teams were out on air marshal missions.

Agents, when not on air marshal missions, conducted inspections of the airports and airlines, as assigned by the Civil Aviation Security Field Office (CASFO) Manger. Each inspection was mandatory, so if you were away, another agent would perform the inspection for you. But when cases developed from those inspections they were reassigned back to the agents responsible for the airport or airline. This meant you always had cases waiting for you when you came off a mission.

I wasn't behind schedule yet, but I was getting close and it was my first day back in the office.

"Gosh, Maggie your inbox was empty when you left ten days ago, but it sure as heck isn't empty now. It feels so good to be loved," I said to no one in particular.

For the next two weeks I researched, wrote, and completed case after case in an attempt finish up everything that had collected in my in-box while I was in Haiti. Overtime was never authorized for report writing so you just had to 'get it done' after each mission. Coupled with inspections, it was a hectic time, but work wasn't always fun.

"That's why 'work' is a four letter word." I said to Agent Stanton on Friday morning.

In the few short years I had been working with the Federal Government it seemed that most emergencies or procedural changes occurred on Fridays-both good and bad. It's as if no one could decide what to do until the end of the week-then it became an emergency-and had to be done immediately!

True to form, just before quitting time, Supervisor Drake called Agent Stanton, Big Earl, and me into his office to notify us that we had been scheduled for another mission. This time we were heading back to Asia for two weeks.

"Ah, Asia in September," Agent Stanton said.

"Yeah, just be sure to have your case work, inspections, and checkpoint testing done, since we're bumping up on the end of the fiscal year. And D.C. doesn't seem to remember or care if field agents, yes you guys, have field work to get done too." Drake responded with a grumble that bordered on a complaint.

Drake was tall, nondescript, and plain looking, with thinning brown hair. He, always stooped slightly when he stood or walked and looked like an old man years before his fiftieth birthday. You could tell he didn't exercise, the slight bulge around his belt revealed that. Yet despite his glasses, his eyes were the only real indicator that he was alive and paying attention to the world around him; for his eyes were strikingly brown, alert, and always evaluating any object that came within his vision.

He certainly always looked angry at the world and his barking voice indicated that for some reason he probably was.

Dismissing us like unruly employees, he barked, "Enjoy your weekend; see you all on Monday."

Unlike Supervisor Drake, we were happy campers. On the road again-well airways-airways to new adventures! YES!

In preparation for the mission to Asia, the next ten days were spent as if we were trying to compete with the Peregrine Falcon, the fastest flying bird found in the United States. Our lives were a world wind of activity.

"I'm exhausted." I muttered at I sipped my first cup of steaming hot cup of coffee while looking out the tiny window over my kitchen sink early on Friday morning.

"One more day in the office Maggie, and you're off again." I said as I turned away from the window to finish up getting ready for work.

Getting ready for work I thought about Supervisor Drake. For some unknown reason he seemed in an unusually foul mood all week, of which I couldn't understand since he usually was pretty grumpy, but it was a steady, even grumpy that you got use to very quickly. So something was eating at him but whatever it was he wasn't sharing.

"Let's not increase his grumpiness by being late." And with that remark, I was out the door, in my beloved Jeep, and off to work.

When I arrived at the office, of course, Agent Stanton was already there, and so was Big Earl. They were both at Kelly's desk. I quickly went and put my briefcase down and walked over to join them.

"Hi ya Maggie," Kelly said with her engaging and happy smile.

"Hi, how's it going Kelly and what's happening?" I said.

"I'm just finishing up with all of your airline tickets, travel orders, and hotel information," she said. "I asked these guys to take a second look at everything and make sure the trip dates, locations, stuff looked right."

With coffee cups in hand, we read and re-read the documents that Kelly handed us. We were all leaving on Sunday night for the first leg of our trip from LAX to Narita, Japan. Our initial secure conference call briefings had taken place yesterday, so after reviewing our documents and giving Kelly the thumbs-up, we were ready to travel.

Arriving at the Tom Bradley International Terminal at LAX Sunday evening we proceeded to begin the check-in and pre-boarding process.

"Greetings," Agent Lopez said to me as I walked up to the small group already gathering near the United Airlines ticket counter.

"Hey there, we meet again."

"Hope everyone is on time this time." He said with a smile, but a serious gleam shimmered in his big brown eyes.

I stepped aside and began my mental checklist of what I had in my carry-on bag: three or four paperbacks that I routinely take with me, notepaper, pen, and of course my firearm, ammo, and knife. As I was going through my checklist I could feel my facial features beginning to take on their standard pre-mission look of "Don't mess with me," as a slight scowl began emerging.

The station manager on duty met us near the end of the ticket counter and asked each of us to follow him. His sole responsibility was to facilitate getting us beyond the screening checkpoint, introduce us to the flight crew team, and then get us onboard the aircraft with as little visibility as possible. We usually planned to pre-board about an hour before scheduled departure time because the additional time onboard would allow us to search the aircraft and get acquainted with the of the interior of the aircraft.

Once behind the airport ticket counters, you enter into a world that is entirely different than what the passengers and family members see. This terminal had recently been remodeled so the furniture didn't look as tired, dirty, or worn as seen in other parts of LAX. And the paint shades were very similar in color, texture, and floor accents. It was actually pretty darn nice and I bet the crews, and crowds of airline employees that passed through these halls and office spaces barely noticed! Most of them were much too busy trying to get flights out on time, looking for lost baggage, occasional animals, and in general making sure that the traveling public was content.

Once we boarded, completed our aircraft search, we quietly took our assigned seats. I was in economy again, but I didn't really mind. The aisle seats were comfortable enough and I could endure a nine and a half hour flight without much trouble anymore. By now I was getting pretty seasoned, downright knowledgeable, on how to get comfortable in a B-747 seat!

I'm a pro, no matter what, it will be okay. I thought as I sat down and put my backpack under the seat in front of me, pushing it all the way forward and to the left so I'd have plenty of room for my feet. I took one of my books out before securing my backpack and placed it in the seat pocket in front of me and then I slowed myself down and began to watch as people began boarding the aircraft.

I spent the first fifteen minutes watching people looking at their boarding passes then at the rows of seats as they tried to figure out where they were sitting. Passengers began struggling to get their luggage swung up over their heads and into the overhead bins. Finally I watched them crawling over people to get into their seats, squirming and settling in with purses, bags, books, and magazines, anything to make them comfortable and occupied for the long flight ahead.

A woman with a young girl, about six years old stopped in front of my row, and I stood to let them in beside me. *No open middle seat for me this trip,* I said to myself as I smiled at the little girl with hair that was shiny, smooth, and very straight.

The little girl looked at me, but didn't return the smile. If fact, as she passed between me, stumbling over and then stepping on my feet, she stuck her pink tongue out at me!

All right, I might be able to endure uncomfortable seats, lousy airline food, and absolutely no sleep for nine hours, I muttered in my head, *but kids, well this is a new one for me.*

This was a typical airline experience sitting beside a six year old for a nine hour flight. Before landing in Narita, I had developed one heck of a headache, and I had goopy strawberry yogurt splattered across my lap and left sleeve of my coat jacket.

This in-flight explosion of food had occurred about two hours before we landed, shortly after we were served breakfast. While the yogurt was quietly riding along with us, it had built up a slight pressure, ready to burst at the seams I suspect at the passenger who was seated in the middle seat in front of the small squirming girl sitting beside me. She, with her fidgety small feet must have kicked the seat thousands of times during our passage across the skies to Asia.

Too many times to count now, the upset man had popped up from his seat and pleaded with the little girl, her mother, and even gave me an emotional plea, begging that someone control the little girls actions. Call button rang, mother scolded, but the kicking never stopped.

I have hand cuffs. I wonder how they work on feet. Was the evil thought that crossed my mind, but I never said a peep. I just watched, tried to read, and tried to look totally like I wasn't fazed a bit.

However, after the strawberry yogurt breakfast splattered across me like an eruption of a volcano I knew I had had enough. I was ready to get off this flight, get away from these passengers, and take a long run along the rice patties just outside of town, and then find a nice glass of chilled chardonnay.

It was time to find solace, freedom, fresh air, a place to run, and to call Dave.

During the bus ride to the Radisson Hotel, arrangements for dinner and for where and when we would meet to debrief from today's flight were finalized.

"I'm not even going to ask what you're going to do after our debriefing," Agent Stanton said, while jabbing Big Earl and smiling over at me in the seat across the aisle from them.

"Yes, as usual, I'm passing on dinner. I know, I know, don't say it, 'I'm so boring', but I've got to run today. And see this yogurt guys? I've got to run off the memory of how I got this all over my clothes," I said.

"Yep, and we can smell it too." Big Earl said as his nose crinkled up.

"The only way to regroup after a mission like that is to run," I said with my voice full of conviction.

"Go for it girl." Big Earl said, "I'm heading for the Gioizza Bar again for some pot stickers, a big bowl of rice, and a few Kirin beers to wash everything down with," as he patted his oversize belly.

"And I'm joining him for a few beers," Agent Stanton chimed in.

I laughed and turned my head and looked out the window as traveled the short fifteen minute drive from the airport to our hotel.

"If I get back in time, I'll come find you because I'm going to need a glass of wine."

Our teams always stayed at the same hotel in Narita. The Radisson Hotel was your typical-looking, high-rise, American-style hotel. The lobby was modern with onsite dining, a business center, indoor and outdoor swimming pool, and two saunas.

The rooms were tiny, the bathroom even tinier, but having a private bathroom was wonderful. A "Yukata", a light weight cotton robe, hung on a clothing hook behind the bathroom door for each guest to use. After so many hours of flying I found this to be a very gracious, welcoming, and delightful luxury for this weary traveler. But first-things-first, I needed to get a run in before I could relax.

The second treat was that the hotel was very close to the Sakura-no-Yama Hill and Naritasan Shinshoji Temples. I knew I could follow the small road from the hotel along the rice paddies to those two temples and back. It was peaceful and gorgeous.

During my first visit here I was given a small map that showed the route for a run that was about four miles round trip. Happily I knew where to go and about how long my run would take.

Once our team met, and our team leader was satisfied that he had collected all of the information he needed for Washington, D.C., we were dismissed for the day.

Racing back up three flights of stairs to my room, I quickly changed, and raced back down to the lobby.

I need this today Maggie, I need this run. I thought as I bolted down the tiny road in the late afternoon sun, headed for the rice patties.

I ran, running as if I was a part of the wind, my pace smooth, strong, even, as my feet quietly touched the pavement until I reached the end of town. When the roads turned to dirt, soft, brown, rich, beautiful dirt I ran, ran, and ran, feeling freer and freer with each passing mile.

Two weeks passed and we were closed to heading home. By then we had flown to and from Seoul, Narita, Singapore, Hong Kong, and Manila. We had one more leg to go, well actually two. Our flight originated out of LAX, but the trip was going to finish at San Francisco International Airport. From there, those of us that lived in Los Angeles would hop a flight home on a regional carrier as regular paying passengers. We'd be in mission status, but without our firearms on our persons, they'd be carried as checked baggage. Federal regulations are as confusing to government employees as they are to the public sometimes, but there wasn't a darn thing we could do about it.

Finally, after nine and a half hours of flying and bumping along across the Pacific ocean, we landed in San Francisco, touched our feet on American soil after two weeks and a couple of days, cleared U.S. customs, and secured our firearms into our hard-sided suitcases for our flights home.

CHAPTER 5

Mellon Man

Big Earl, Agent Stanton, and I looked like hell when Supervisor Yuen met us at baggage claim. It wasn't a social call; it was his way of ensuring that his agents were home and that they would be reporting into work the following day.

"Has anybody ever asked that guy what's up with the checking on his employees?" Big Earl asked as we walked towards our gate to catch our flight to LA.

"Beats me" I said.

"Welcome to the federal government," Agent Stanton said, "And yes, you've officially met a bureaucrat."

I chuckled because I knew we truly had.

As we stood in line to board the Southwest Airlines flight, we yawned, rocked side to side, tapped our feet on the carpet, and for-the-most-part did what we could to stay awake until we boarded the aircraft. Once onboard we would tuck our carry-on gear away, put on our seat belts and slept during the one hour and ten minute flight home.

Southwest Airlines is known for three things: on time departures, funny flight attendants, and open seating. Open seating meaning once you are in the aircraft you are on your own to find a seat. The closer you were in front of the line at boarding, the better chances you had of getting an aisle or a window seat.

"I know, I know, this flight isn't very long, but I sure would like to get an aisle seat for my ride home." I said to my fellow agents.

"Yep, I know the feeling," Big Earl said. "Putting this 250 pound frame into any airline seat is tough, but a middle seat, well forget about it. It's almost impossible," his deep raspy voice boomed out, as he smiled and patted his stomach.

Onboard I couldn't believe my luck. Very close to the front of the aircraft was an aisle seat. I quickly sat down as Big Earl and Stanton passed by me in search of seats further back in the aircraft.

I could feel myself slowing down; my eye lids were beckoning for me rest.

"Hold on, hold on. Just a little longer," I quietly told myself as if soothing a newborn.

Settling in, I pulled out my Runner's Magazine and thumbed to the page that I had dog-eared earlier to mark my spot. I loved running, so much that I usually devoured the entire content of the magazine in one sitting.

Even though I was off-duty, I kept a watchful eye on the cockpit door, the main aircraft entry, and the passengers boarding. This flight appeared to be completely booked.

Shortly before the forward door closed, a man rushed by me, saying, in a distraught and loud voice, "I'm not sitting by that man!"

Instantly switching into full alert mode, I looked forward to see the man flailing his arms, shaking his head back and forth, and rapidly speaking with the flight attendant that was standing between him and the cockpit door.

Getting out of my seat, I walked towards them. "Hi, I'm Maggie Stewart, FAA Security. Is something wrong?" I said in a low voice, as I showed the flight attendant my Special Agent credentials.

"Yes, there is," the flight attendant said. Then the man said, "I'm not sitting next to a drunk guy," as he pointed towards the back of the aircraft.

A second flight attendant joined us and said that she just walked past the man and he seemed okay-quiet, but yes, she could smell the alcohol on him, as she passed his seat.

"Is there another seat for me?" asked the man dressed in a business suit, with his briefcase and newspaper.

"I don't have any carry-on luggage, I'm flying to Los Angeles for a business meeting, and I'll be back later tonight." He said, as if not having any luggage was going to help him secure another seat.

"No sir, we are completely booked." The flight attendant said. "I'm very sorry, but that is the only seat available."

I looked at the three of them, and made a decision.

"I'll switch with you," I said.

The flight attendants looked surprised and relieved at the same time.

"It's okay, I'll be able to keep an eye on him." I said.

I walked back to my seat, grabbed my backpack and magazine, and headed towards the back of the aircraft.

"I should have known Maggie that a middle seat had my name on it after all," I muttered under my breath.

Smiling, I nodded, and climbed over the man in the aisle seat, as best I could, and looked at the man no one wanted to sit by. He nodded at me, but didn't speak. Smelling stale alcohol and sweat, I wondered how much he had been drinking.

Briefing looking to the back of the aircraft before I sat down, I saw Big Earl and Agent Stanton were sitting a few rows behind me so I knew if all hell broke loose at least I'd have back-up. The three of us made eye contact, indicating that they knew a situation had occurred and they were there to back me up if needed.

It's good to have friends behind me, literally. I thought.

Unfortunately, there we're any restrictions on how much alcohol a person could consume either before boarding or on an aircraft. The flight attendants could stop selling liquor to a passenger, but I can't recall in all the years that I've been flying that ever happening. It was a concern, I wondered about from time to time, but I figured the revenue source was too lucrative for the airlines to do anything about it.

My thoughts swirled around that, *Perhaps it's time for the FAA to do something about passengers drinking and flying.*

The flight attendants made their final announcements, the forward door closed, and we were ready to taxi, heading to Los Angeles.

Once we lifted off, the stale alcohol smelling man looked over at me.

"Hey, how's it going?" I said.

"Not great," he grumbled.

"I'm Maggie." I said as I extended my hand to shake his.

"I'm Ruben."

"Yikes", I thought to myself. His hand was enormous, maybe the size of a small cantaloupe. It felt rough and gritty like a cantaloupes skin. His arms looked like suntanned palm tree. I could tell that he was tall, probably over 6 feet and outweigh me by close to one hundred pounds. I usually pray at the beginning of each flight for safe passage, but for this trip I decided to pray for the entire trip.

Gosh, if he decides to punch me, I'm dead. I thought.

"What's taking you to L.A.?" I asked.

Ruben grunted, "I'm a long shore man and I'm trying to catch-up with my ship. She left yesterday from Oakland heading for the Port of Los Angeles. I was supposed to board her yesterday, but I went out, tied one on, and missed her."

"Well that doesn't sound good." I replied. "What happens now?"

"If I miss the ship, I'm screwed," is all he quietly mumbled with his head hung low.

The flight attendant pushing a drink cart past us looked at me and mouthed the words thank you.

Ruben fell asleep for a better part of the flight after our brief conversation. As for me, I was fully awake. I finished reading my magazine, passed on drinks, and waited to arrive in L.A. Fortunately, "melon man" was asleep so the temptation for him to drink anymore rolled past us without incident.

After landing, everyone scrambled to retrieve their carry-on items in an attempt to get off the aircraft quickly. Ruben stood and grabbed his bag from the overhead as we slowing inched forward towards freedom.

"Who are you, a cop?" Ruben asked.

"Me? Why?" I asked with a cautious inflection.

"Seems like there's been a lot of chatter and eye contact with the stewardess." He said with a hint of distrust in his voice, his hands beginning to curl into fists.

"Well I know them, I fly a lot, and these commuter flights usually have the same crew on them. After awhile you get recognized, for good or for bad, it happens."

Ruben grunted, "I don't like cops," as we continued our slow move forward, which by now wasn't fast enough for me. Glancing back, I saw Big Earl taking in the conversation, but there was little hope he could help me since he was three rows behind and the aisles were now jammed with anxious passengers wanting to escape the confines of this aircraft as much as I did.

At the front of the aircraft, as Ruben stepped into the jet way, the flight attendant again thanked me for switching seats. Saying it was no problem I deplaned with an enormous sigh of relief.

Once I was in the terminal, Big Earl and Agent Stanton appeared at my side.

"What was that all about?" Big Earl asked.

"Well you know, sometimes we're hired to protect, and some-times we're hired to defend – defend ourselves that is. Let's just say, that it was my day to defend myself... well almost."

As we walked to collect our checked baggage, I told them the story of Melon Man versus Mad Dog.

CHAPTER **6**

Hey I'm Back

Being back in Marana, Airzona, was not only a walk down memory lane, but the place where everything began, the origins of my career, my ability to protect, along with being the place that always proved to be a continual challenge of wits, strength, determination, and drive for me. Standing on the firing line; once again, I could feel the inside of my mouth getting sticky and growing as dry as the dusty desert surrounding me. My ear and eye gear protecting me from the brass that would soon be flying around me. I couldn't escape the rapid beating of my heart that was pounding like a tidal wave inside my Dave Clark ear protectors.

Calm down, Maggie, I'm not alone: twenty-five of us are here for our two week semi-annual recurrent federal air marshal training. You think I'd all be use to this after five years of flying, training, flying, and then-what a surprise-more training. "But heck no, once again I'm buzzing with anticipation, and nerves." I said under my breath. As I peeked at my fellow agents, before the drill began, I could see we were all are waiting in anticipation for Kevin, our range instructor to start the drill.

It was time has come to get ready for flying brass-hot bullets-flying by me. Flying brass? I'm a lefty, so I shoot left-handed. When everyone is lined up on the firing line ready to commence firing, the right-handed shooters are a few inches away from my extended left firing arm. This scenario always allows me to have the pleasure of being a little closer to the recoil action and noise of the shooter on my left. Unfortunately for me, that also means to the flying brass that sometimes smacks into my protective glasses or flies down the front of my shirt. Either place it's landed, hot flying brass is not what you want burning you on qualification day.

Firearms qualifications consisted of shooting paper silhouette targets from close range, double taping to the head, single tapping to the main body, then moving back further and further away from the targets as instructed by the range master. All positions of firing are timed, and accuracy is not only critical, but expected. It's pretty much demanded that all of your ammo finds the bulls-eye of your target each and every time. No patterned targets allowed, just one neat little hole. A hole that grows larger and larger as the bullets hit the paper with precision. Precision meaning that you will and can accurately, with consistently, hit the kill zone.

The pace was rapid-fire and move, rapid-fire, move again. We moved as a team, a single entity, farther and farther away from the five-yard line until we were standing at the twenty-five yard mark. Precision was critical, equally at the five and twenty-five yard lines because we were training to protect the lives of passengers and crew member's inside airplanes. Each shot had to be perfect because shooting inside an airplane meant accuracy was very crucial because making a mistake inside a 'tin can', fondly referred to as an aircraft, was not highly recommended.

Screaming out our names, our range master told us which lane to go to. I was ordered to go stand behind the three-yard line at lane number twelve. Big Earl was on my left and Georgia was on my right. Our weapons were holstered, our now-sweaty hands, or at least mine, were at our sides, eye and ear protection in place, and additional clips of ammunition accessible on our belts. As we lined up, I could only hear my heartbeat pounding away in my ears. *So this is it. Here we go again, Maggie Stewart, just stay calm, move faster than your normal turtle's pace and forget about everything else. It's all going to be just fine.*

The range master shouted "Fire in the hole," and the starting gun went off. Within split second, shots roared as twelve semi-automatics went off simultaneously. Hot casing went flying everywhere, hitting the ground in front, behind, and beside us like hot raindrops. You could hear them sizzling as they flew through the air hitting the pavement.

"Cease fire and holster your weapons," commanded the range master. We were directed to the next firing position and again shots rang out. I was too nervous to look at my target. I kept my eyes to the ground, ensuring that my firearm was in a safe position before we were directed to holster them and move to our next position. We all moved quietly and with precision. This process was repeated five times in rapid succession, giving us barely enough time to breathe in the warm sage-scented desert air.

Like the ever repeating Groundhog's Day, our annual qualifications day, happened over, and over, but now it was finished. Everyone was again commanded to holster their firearms, and when the range master called the line safe we walked down to the three-foot firing line and stood with our hands at our sides waiting for Kevin to score our targets. The wait was grueling, but in reality we could tell quickly by the target positioning if we were going to qualify or not. The closer the bullet holes were to the bull's-eye, the higher your score.

One of the agents started to walk down range to look at his target and Kevin yelled again, "Stand down, and holster your weapons NOW." As he walked briskly up to the agent and began shouting, "Are you an idiot? What the hell do you think you're doing? Get off my range, now!" The stunned agent mumbled something back which appeared to really tick Kevin off, and the agent was ordered off the range for good.

Welcome to recurrent training, I said to myself.

What a way to start the week. One agent disqualified and twenty-four more counting their blessings, watching the seconds drip by, hoping that by days end it wasn't them that had to leave the range.

Full of dust, sweat, and attitude, I finished up my three mile run for the day and headed back to my room to get cleaned up. I gazed at the nearby mountain range and sighed. I hiked there often, seeking the sanctuary of the cool air. But this was a short trip, just a week, so hiking in the nearby mountains would have to wait.

I was glad Georgia was here so we could release our anxieties over a couple of glasses of wine at night while recalling what happened that day. It would be great to catch-up on all the news and gossip too.

Walking into the bar at 6 P.M., I immediately knew a lot of "happy hour" had already taken place. As soon as I stepped through the door frame and into the semi-dark and dusty bar, hoots and hollers swept over me like a tidal wave.

Okay, Maggie, my pals are in high gear already. Let's see what kind of trouble we can all get into tonight. I walked up to Big Earl, who simultaneously handed me a bowl of popcorn and a glass of wine.

"Do I ever love you," I shouted over the blasting country music, shouts, and laughter that filled the bar. "You are the best," I said while muscling in between him and another fellow agent sitting on a bar stool next to him.

"Glad you could make it to the party." He shouted. "I'm glad this day is over. Firearms and fitness all is one day makes me drink beer."

"Me too," I hollered back. "Cheers!"

"I heard we're doing some tactical training with knives tomorrow."

Big Earl nodded in the affirmative, "Yep, that's what I heard too."

I downed my first glass of wine pretty quickly while hogging an entire bowl of popcorn to myself.

With my second glass of wine in hand, I left Big Earl who was talking politics to the agent next to him and found Georgia, Bob, and Morris. They were sitting at a table deep in conversation about something too. Everyone was laughing and smiling so I knew they had to be telling lies!

"Hey guys, how's it going?" I pulled up a chair and sat down.

"Great now that qualifications are over for the week." Georgia said as she held her beer bottle up, signaling a toast was in order.

"Here, here!" Everyone said as if on cue.

Morris told us his version of how he was almost kicked out of the air marshal program a few months ago by almost missing a trip. I knew all about it. He should have missed it, because I was onboard that day when he came running up our aircraft as the forward door was being closed. What I didn't know was that he had gotten written up, suspended for two weeks, and would not be getting a promotion this year.

I have to admit, I thought he was a total chump, but he did seem contrite. Well kind of. He was now that he'd been taken to the mat by management. I was silently amazed that management did anything at all. In federal government, management seemed to take action on things that didn't matter and didn't take action on things that did. It would take a lot of paperwork to get Morris fired, so I wondered why anyone bothered.

During the past three years I've learned that once you got hired, make it through your first year of employment, it was almost impossible to get rid of bad performers. Unless they committed a capital crime, got arrested, convicted, and got sentenced to jail. But even then it takes awhile for bureaucratic wheels to start moving.

As I sat and listened to Morris' self-serving story, I started to get impatient and I wanted to slug this moron.

I was more than ready to escape this conversation of excuses and incompetence. He gloated that he saved his own skin by talking his way out of almost missing his flight to a manager that didn't fly as an air marshal and didn't give a damn about our program since it took staff hours away from his office.

Ah, I bet the bean-counter manager punished him so he could have him around to get more inspection work done. I said to myself in disgust. I was learning more about the political machine and I knew I didn't like it very much. But I loved my job, I loved protecting travelers, and I loved my fellow cadre. So it was time to escape this conversation and call it a night.

When Morris finished pontificating about how he had mitigated his situation down to the point of keeping his job, I piped in saying, "The problem with you saving your job is that if there's ever a fire fight on a mission we'd be one member down if you didn't show. And you almost didn't-that's the point-you didn't care enough to be on time. There's no radio call for back up at 350,000 feet. It's us against the bad guy. So next time, I'd personally appreciate it if you'd show up."

I pushed my chair back, stood up, and with a tinge of anger I said, "Night, I'm out of here."

"Hey, you can't talk to me like that." Morris yelled, standing up, and point a finger at me.

"I just did you moron." I turned, putting my back between him and the door as I walked away.

As I stormed into the cool evening night and looked up towards the stars as I breathed a sigh of relief that I was free of the noise, the ego posturing, and ever consuming male attitude of Morris.

Disregard my previous thoughts Maggie about cutting his some slack, he's a moron.

I half ran, half danced back to my room, in an attempt to shake off the melancholy that was seeping into my soul. I didn't like incompetence in any shape or form.

I had been born into a family of structure. I joined the military where I experienced even more structure. Then I went to work for an airline where structure was critical for safety, on time departures and arrivals. And now within the Federal Aviation Administration; specifically the air marshal program, where structure was imperative to saving lives. I was living a structured life to the fullest now. I couldn't escape structure.

And unfortunately, I didn't escape the creeping sadness, but I did manage to capture a few night-flying bugs, that stuck against my face, neck, and bare arms as I moved through their flight paths. Cursing out loud, I stumbled into my room as I swatted off the last bug from my face.

When I got to our classroom the next morning, the team was advised that we'd be spending the rest of the week in the gym. We'd be practicing various knife take away techniques that were being taught by an instructor from the FBI. We were the first trainees taking this course and it would be a learning curve for both the instructor and the trainees. We'd be required to learn the skill set with a pass or fail grade.

The next three days were spent in the gym learning how to kill people with knives and practicing how to take knives away from enemies. We stabbed, jabbed, pounded, pinched, flipped, poked, and beat the snot out of our opponents for hours until we were told it was over.

"Stabbing or getting stabbed is what it's all about this week, Maggie." I said, "And it just can't get any better than this!"

My wrists were black and blue from being struck so many times by my mock opponents, who in some cases gleefully chopped at my wrists with the meaty part of their hands. The objective was to find the nerves that ran under the skin that involuntarily cause the opponent to drop the knife. But since we were learning, we'd miss the nerve, and cause bruising instead.

"Okay, you're done. Good job agents. This module of training is complete and you are all dismissed." The FBI instructor said with no fan fair whatsoever.

"Well, I can take a hint." I said to Georgia, as I got up from the gym mat I was sitting on, rubbing my wrists as I walked towards the mess hall for lunch.

"Such personality, it's been a lovely week hasn't it?" retorted Georgia.

"It was splendid, without a doubt. Painful, but splendid," I said while rubbing my wrists.

After lunch, we finished up in the classroom with a final exam and the required recertification paperwork that needed to be completed after every stay at Marana. By the week's end no one grumbled about the paperwork, we were all just happy to be done with training for another year. Our training began with twenty-five agents and we ended with twenty-four. Once again, I was very proud to be one of the graduates.

Since my beloved Jeep was in the shop, I had been forced to rent a car. I reserved an inexpensive company car, but was upgraded to a red sleek convertible. My car was packed and I was ready for the trip back home.

As I turned onto Interstate 10, heading North, I once again left Marana in the rear view mirror. I-10 would take me to the 91 West, and I'd be home in no time.

Out on the open road, as I passed through the Sonora Desert, pressing my foot harder and harder on the accelerator to see what this little, red beauty could do. The warm desert air whipped through my hair and I watched the desert speed past me. I couldn't remember the last time I drove so fast, but I soon remembered what an Adeline rush was. As I hit 100 MPH, the flashing lights of a highway patrol car began tracking behind me.

"Crap, guess I should have slowed down. Now you've gone and done it Maggie." I pulled over, grabbed my credential case where my California driver's license was and waited.

Once I stopped, the Highway Patrol officer sat in his car for a few minutes before moving towards my vehicle. I knew he was gathering information about my rental car and perhaps allowing me to get a little more nervous than I already was.

Standing beside my car, the officer said, "Good afternoon. Hand me your license and registration please."

"Here's my license, but the registration is in the glove box. May I get that?" I asked.

What are you thinking you girl, you're okay, you'll probably get a ticket, but you're the 800 pound gorilla. This guy is just CHP. Calm down. You've got this, just chill.

"Give me your rental contract, and tell me why you were in such a hurry?" the officer asked.

"I'm heading home. I've been at Marana all week. I'm sorry it's totally my fault officer." I clearly stated. I'm *a dumb ass I am.* I said to myself.

"What are you doing at Marana? Are you a fed?" he asked.

"Yes. I'm a Federal Air Marshal. I've been out in Marana finishing up firearms, tactical, and self-defense training."

"Let me see your badge and credential." The now semi-friendlier officer said, "And step out of the car."

I handed him my credentials, unbuckled my seat belt, and stepped out of the car onto the hot pavement.

"Wait here." He instructed as he walked back towards his squad car.

Oh boy, I screw up. I just want to go home.

When the officer had completed what he needed to accomplish he strode over, handed me my credentials and smiled.

"I can see by your legs that you must be a runner. Me too! Your license information checks out. So as a professional law enforcement courtesy I suggest in the future, at least when you're here in Arizona, that if you want to keep your license, you slow down. Have a nice day!"

"I most certainly will sir. Thank you."

Getting back into my car I knew I was one was a very lucky duck.

CHAPTER 7

What A Surprise

I pulled up to my apartment five and a half hours later. It was dark, I was hungry and tired, but most of all, I needed a shower. My body was layered with dirt, grit, grim, oil, and salt, topped with fiery sunburn that made my skin red and painful to touch. My butt and lower back were sore from sitting in the car. When I got home I looked like a little, old lady. I felt like one too.

As I stepped into my little cottage, turning on the light, I headed for the refrigerator to get a cold glass of wine. I was very, very happy to have sanctuary in this beach oasis once again. I felt like a swallow returning to find her nest still intact after being gone for a season…and it was wonderful!

There wasn't much food in the house, so I nibbled on crackers and cheese, and a second glass of wine. I showered, poked through my mail, and crawled into bed before midnight.

I slept like the dead only to be woken early the next morning by my neighbors' bird. Squawking away, Bill's parrot-perched on his left shoul-der-chattered on as they left for one of their traditional early morning walks along the beach strand. Bill's parrot was always a good indicator that it was the weekend because they only walked on Saturday and Sunday mornings because Bill, like most people, worked.

Once my morning ritual of savoring a steaming cup of coffee was finished I decided it was time to get outside and go for a run. The strand was just a block from my house so there was no excuse to not run. The view was spectacular: miles virtually unlimited, and hundreds of places along the way to stop and take a break. It was the perfect location for running especially for distance training. I still was on track to run the Palos Verdes Marathon early next year.

Let's go! I grabbed a bottle of water, half a toasted, unbuttered bagel, a stick of gum, and I was out the door for my ten-mile run. I planned to run north, passed the Redondo Beach pier, the Hermosa Beach pier, to just south of the Manhattan Beach pier and back. It is a long, flat course that runs adjacent to the beach, except in one spot by the old power plant in Redondo Beach. It's traffic free, flat, with plenty of bathrooms, and drinking fountains along the way.

An hour and a half later I was just about home. As I turned the corner onto Camino La Costa, running as fast as I could along the final block, I saw a man sitting on my front steps.

"Dave!" I shouted and ran even faster into his open arms. "What are you doing here? I thought you were in Miami or the Caribbean somewhere?"

"When we got back to Dallas, we were supposed to do one more turn-around but the freight wasn't ready, so we're off until Tuesday. Since I was already packed, I figured you wouldn't mind if I came out. Besides, I can't get you off my mind Maggie." With that said our eyes met and then he kissed me. A long, lingering kiss that left me weaker in the legs than my run did.

Dave nuzzled my bare shoulder. "Let's go inside," he said. Then his mouth brushed my earlobe. We locked eyes again for a heartbeat and quickly escaped the neighbors gawking by going into my tiny cottage apartment.

We kissed again, our tongues touched, and our kiss deepened. Dave's hands were at my waist, mine on his shoulders, and then we were pressing into each other.

Our clothes started coming off. *Forget taking a shower.* Fleeted through my head. *Later, Maggie, later.*

Dave scooped me up, carried me into my bedroom and dropped me on my bed. He quickly stripped off the rest of his clothes, all the while watching me with his piercing blue eyes. His hands were ever so steady, but his breathing was ragged, as if he'd just finished running.

The following morning I awoke in a tangle of damp sheets and next to Dave. We'd made a serious dent in the condom supply, and I was feeling very, very relaxed. Dave stirred beside me, and I snuggled into him.

"Mmm," he whispered. "Nice."

And the love making began again. Two hours later, and a few condoms less, we both were thinking that sex was an excellent thing, but we needed coffee, food, and showers.

"I'll start the coffee Love, if you want to start the shower." I said as I dragged myself out of bed. This sex goddess was more than a trifle sore, but my-oh-my it was so worth it.

Yum, I thought to myself.

We took a shower, got dressed, and ambled towards the kitchen. We poured our coffee and sat outside. The patio wasn't very private, as it was open, and faced the street, but it had a better view and ocean breeze than other patio in the back.

I stooped and picked up the Daily Breeze newspaper that I subscribed to and handed it to him. As he sat drinking his coffee and reading the paper, I smiled. I smiled at his rumpled clothes, slightly messy hair, and five o'clock shadow. The back door was open, and the morning sea breeze blew though my tiny apartment, so it was cool and marvelous.

Dave drained his coffee and continued to read the paper.

I found myself wanting to refill his coffee mug. Along with wanting to cook him breakfast, do his laundry, and sleep with him every night. I was hooked.

Dave looked over at me and smiled. I could tell he knew exactly what I was thinking.

I blushed a deep, deep pink, and I felt the heat in my cheeks.

"We'll have to do something about this one day, my dear Maggie." He said and he leaned over to kiss me.

"I sure hope so." I said as I got up to refill our coffee mugs, kissing him on top of his head as I walked by.

"Missy, let's go to the Chart House for dinner tonight," Dave said. "I've got to get back to Dallas tomorrow and work, so let's go have a really nice dinner tonight."

"Okay, that sounds like a date to me. I can't wait."

The Chart House in Redondo Beach is right on the water's edge, in fact more because it's built on pilings extended into the ocean. When you sit at a window seat you can see the surf crashing just a few feet below you, and the Brown Pelicans swooping in occasionally to catch their evening meal fresh from the sea.

That night, we dined on plates of exquisite salad, cold and crisp with blue cheese dressing, steak and lobster, fine red wine and a zambucca liquor, whole coffee beans for our after dinner liquor.

"This had been a marvelous dinner, Honey," I cooed. "Our evening has been simply perfect in every single way. I love you, Dave."

Woops, I didn't mean for that four letter word to slip out. Yikes, I said to myself.

"Yes, its perfect, my dear Maggie. And, the only thing that could make it really perfect," Dave, said while getting down on one knee, "is if you'll marry me?"

"Yes, yes, I will marry you." We kissed as everyone clapped and cheered around us to share in our joy.

When we got home I couldn't wait to call my sister. "Sis, proposed, he got down on one knee and proposed right there in the restaurant. He proposed. I'm going to get married Sis!"

"I'm so happy for the two of you," she said. "I love you sis."

"I love you too. I had to tell you first, but now I better call Mom and our brother Tim," I said. "Love you, bye."

After waiting six months, my transfer from the Los Angeles office to the Dallas office was approved. I had submitted paperwork for a hardship relocation request which meant the move was completely on my own time and my financial responsibility, but I didn't mind. I wanted to begin my life living with my darling Dave. And, I wanted to start a family soon. I was twenty-six years old now and the clock was beginning to tick.

It's time for babies. It's time to start a family. I thought as I picked up the phone to call Dave. *Whoa, whoa, whoa, too early to think this, I'm engaged, but not married yet.*

"Honey, Honey, my transfer came through Effective June 1st," I gushed into the phone. "Six weeks from now we'll be together."

"What do you think about getting married before you transfer Missy? I want you to be my wife sooner than later."

"It would be a dream come true. I love you."

"I love you too Maggie."

On the morning of May 21st, I was a bundle of nerves. Dave and I arranged to be married in Santure, Puerto Rico, during one of his turn-arounds! He was in between flights! For us, time was running out in a very positive way: my transfer from Los Angeles to Dallas had been approved and I was schedule to report in the Dallas office on June 1st.

Dave and I wanted to marry somewhere that had some meaning for us, was near the ocean, and was someplace beautiful. I have lived in St. Croix and Puerto Rico before joining the FAA, and Dave flew in and out of Puerto Rico so we decided to marry there.

"Don't cry, Mom. It's okay, don't cry." I said after the wedding.

"You two look so beautiful, it's hard not to cry," she said through her now stuffy nose.

Part II

CHAPTER 8

And So It Began

"Wow, it's hot," I said to Sylvia as we drove across the Mojave Desert on our way to Texas. Dave had gotten called out on a last minute emergency flight so my sister decided to road trip with me to help me move. We'd have to drive all weekend in order to get my sister back to San Diego for work early Monday morning. But at least we were together.

Our plan was to drive twelve hours Friday and another twelve on Saturday. We'd only spend one night on the road, so we'd arrive in time to get my sister on a flight back to San Diego on Sunday. It was ambitious, but we knew we could do it.

By the time my sister and I were heading east on Interstate 10, the sun had already peaked over the horizon. It was getting warm as we passed through Palm Springs, California towards Phoenix, Arizona.

"Let's aim for getting as close to Las Cruces, New Mexico, as we can today." I said to my sister.

"Sounds like a plan to me," she replied.

'Step By Step' by the New Kids on the block, started playing on the radio and, almost as if on cue, we began singing to the number one hit that summer of June 1990. We sang along, laughing, as my blue Jeep rolled down the interstate towards my beloved husband.

My sister and I are fraternal twins, born five minutes apart, first her and then me. Our father named us names that have no family history whatsoever. Our middle names are those of our great-aunt and grandmother, Nell and Irene, so those names made sense to us, but not our given names. Our brother, who is two years older, is named Timothy Ian with no family ties either, so I guess our dad just liked those names. And our Mom, it appears, had no decision in our names what-so-ever.

I'll have to ask Mom about that next time I talk to her. I muttered to myself.

My twin is a mechanical engineer by profession and is the smartest person I know. She can look at something that is broken and figure out how to repair it in a matter of minutes. She builds things from scratch, taking measurements using hand tools to create whatever she wants. My sister is tough, fun, smart, fit, and my very best friend. So having her along on this road trip was perfect. I was moving away from her again, like I had when I joined the Navy, but our bonds had gotten stronger these past few years since we lived just a little over one hundred miles away from each other. But now I was moving twelve hundred miles away, so I knew we'd be buying a lot of airline tickets to go back and forth between San Diego where she lived, and Dallas where my new home waited.

It's going to be okay, I kept telling myself as I heard the tread of my Jeep tires humming along the hot, black asphalt.

Sylvia totally understood and accepted my moving because she knew what love was all about. She had married her honey, Bernie, last year. It was a simple wedding in the Laguna Mountains, near San Diego, but well attended by both sides of the family. It was a festive event full of laughter, dancing, and of course champagne.

Well beyond dark, we found a hotel just outside Las Cruces, New Mexico.

As I put the car in idle, I exclaimed, "Oh goody, sister we drove 680 miles today!"

"Yes, you've always an over achiever. I can't wait to over achieve tomorrow too!"

After eating greasy hamburgers from the diner next door we walked back to the hotel. We were exhausted, and a little melancholy because we knew this road trip would be ending tomorrow and we'd be traveling our separate ways, into our separated lives once again.

"Night Syl, thanks for all the help driving today." I said as I tucked myself into bed and closed my eyes.

"Glad we're together. Love you. Nite sis."

The hotel room alarm clock blasted with such intensity that it scared the hell out of me. It took me a couple of seconds to figure out where I was.

"Whoa Nelly, that's loud." My sister said as she tapped the release button on top of the alarm clock.

"Yep, that's for sure."

"Let's get out of here and find some coffee."

"Okay sleepy head, glad to see you still love getting up early."

"I only like to get up early when I know I'm going to hike," my sister said while simultaneously throwing a pillow at me.

"Yikes."

Climbing into my Jeep at 5 A.M., hot, steaming coffees in hand, I sang out loud, "We're on the road again, oh yea, on the road again."

"Here's to another long day ahead of us." Sylvia said as we drove out of the nearly full hotel parking lot. "Only you and I would get up before the crows."

Passing through Las Cruces we headed out on Interstate 10 once again towards El Paso. Just outside of town we found Interstate 20 which would begin our northeast drive towards Ft. Worth, Texas. It would be a grueling day of heat and desert, with miles and miles of flat empty land. As we passed Abilene, we could smell the natural gasses being burned off from the oil wells. The air smelt terrible. I could feel the grime and dirt sticking to my skin, clogging up my nostrils, and filling my eyes with grains of desert dust.

"Man-oh-man, I'm missing the ocean breeze, palm trees, and green grass already." I said while driving and peering ahead at the dry, dreary landscape. "I had forgotten how empty and open the Texas landscape is."

My sister looked over at me and shrugged her shoulders. She had no response. No need, the look on her damp, red face told me she was thinking the same thing.

"Oh, the things we do for love."

We arrived in the Fort Worth Metroplex just in time for the 5 P.M. evening traffic. "Well, well, I couldn't have planned this any better."

We still had about thirty-five miles to go to reach the town of Coppell, Texas, where David had found a two bedroom, two bath townhome for us. He had moved from the apartment where he was living to find a bigger place for the two of us. Plus we both wanted to be close to the airport so we didn't have to drive very far to work.

As we crawled along in traffic, I thought about the week ahead and what was about to change; finally living with my sweetie pie, a new office, separation from my sister, brother, my mom, my little beach cottage, and of course separation from the ocean.

"*Big, big changes ahead Maggie.*" My heart was ready. I was ready for love, starting to hear that "baby clock" ticking, ready for marriage, ready for a family of my own.

A few hours later we pulled up to 218 Samuel Blvd., Apartment 5E, my sister and I were more than ready to get out of the car. We weren't sure because our bee-hinds felt permanently glued to the now dirty and damp cloth Jeep seats.

I was dripping with satisfaction that we made it!

"*Mad Dog is a marathon driver.*" I told myself.

"Hello there Missy." Dave yelled as he half ran, half walked down the sidewalk from the townhome.

Big, bear hugs and kisses followed, making the trip worth it. My sister and Dave reintroduced themselves to one another as we grabbed our bags from the back of the Jeep.

"How was the trip? And I'm really sorry I wasn't with you two beautiful ladies, but work was insistent that I take this trip. It was high-end cargo that needed special handling." He told the two of us as Dave and I walked hand and hand into our new home.

The townhome was two stories with a living room, kitchen, small dining area, and half bath downstairs. Upstairs there were two bedrooms with a full bathroom beside the two tinier bedrooms. It was small, but very clean and neat. Every wall was painted Navajo white. The kitchen glistened with white tiles covering the counters. There was even a dishwasher and a washer and drier in a small room off the kitchen. The living room had a fire place, and the windows had white mini-blinds that provided privacy from any passerby in the parking lot. The backdoor led to a small fenced in patio that faced south. Underneath the stairs there was a storage area that you could almost stand-up in with a light.

This will definitely be useful for storage. I thought as I peered through the pint size door. But I didn't have to worry about storage for a few weeks since my furniture and personal belongings were about ten days behind me. What I needed for the next few weeks was packed in the back of the Jeep.

Sadly, Sunday morning came way too quickly. Sylvia and I got up early so we could go for a long walk before her flight. At 6:30 A.M., the air was already hot and sticky. My sister's flight was at 2 P.M., so we had plenty of time to stroll, cups of coffee in hand, and chat. We didn't do this often, stroll, our walked were more like forced marches with my sister setting the pace and me keeping up.

"Remember to walk early." Sylvia said to me. "I know you're not an early bird when it comes to exercise, but it's going to be way too hot to exercise later in the day until you get use to it here."

"I know it's totally different than California that's for sure."

"I miss you already."

"I miss you too."

After walking for nearly an hour we got back to the house, put our empty cups in the sink, and started to get ready to head for the airport. Dave was awake and waiting for us.

"Hi honey, miss us?"

"Sure did Missy."

We planned to leave thirty-minutes early so my sister and I could see where my office was. I had no clue how to get to my new office. I only knew it was on Fuller-Wiser Road and it was on the west-side of the airport. Our townhome was on the north-side of DFW Airport.

Our drive was quiet for all three of us, each involved in our own personal thoughts. I was ecstatic to finally be with my husband, but I was going to miss my sister terribly, and I was a bit apprehensive about transferring to a new office because it was new: new agents, new policies, new airports and airlines to learn.

God Maggie, you don't even know how to get to the office yet! I thought. *I'm going to need a map. Everything is flat here; I don't have the Palos Verdes hill as a landmark to find my way home.*

I glanced at Dave and smiled.

"It's going to be okay, honey," Dave said as he reached over to take my hand in his.

"Yes, I will, but I'm sure going to miss my sister."

"I'll second that," my sister said from the back seat.

The two-story, tan and white building sat all by itself at the top of a sloping street. There was a small non-descript church in a warehouse type building across the street and nothing else. As we walked up to the office door to confirm we were at the right place, departing aircraft roared over head from the multiple runways that were the center piece of activity at the DFW Airport.

"Yep, we're in the right place." Dave said. "I thought this was the security office."

"Good, now at least I sort of know where I'm going Honey, but I think I'm going to need a map for a few days anyway. There aren't any landmarks to help navigate to where I am."

"It looks like a nice office Maggie."

"I think so too. Especially when I figure out how to get here on my own!"

"Well it will get better with time, Honey. I love you and I'm so glad we're finally together." Dave said hugging me, rubbing my back, and giving me a peck on my lips.

"Me too."

"Okay, let's get to the airport; this lady has a flight to catch." Dave said as he smiled at my sister.

Big hugs, wet cheeks, and with long good-byes we got Sylvia to her gate. My sister's eyes grew wide and solemn as we said our goodbyes.

The melancholy building in my heart was unmistakable, but I knew we'd be visiting one another soon enough. We just had to, being twins, it was mandatory. Besides it was only a two and a half hour flight or a twenty-two hour drive. It was very doable by either mode of transportation.

"Bye, I love you guys." My sister said as she walked towards the jet way bridge and handed her ticket to the agent. Once inside the jet way, she turned again and waved before disappearing onto the awaiting aircraft.

"Bye," I yelled, my left arm extending in the air as if I was trying to hold onto her. "I love you."

CHAPTER 9

Meeting the Neighbors

Monday morning, once again, came with a blast of my Sandhill Crane alarm as I awoke with a startle, not fully knowing where I was. My sweetie was asleep, flat on his back, with his mouth slightly open, and I swear he was smiling. I smiled, kissed him on the cheek, grabbed my robe, and slowly walked downstairs to turn on the coffee pot, grab the newspaper that hopefully, was waiting just outside our door.

Glorious! It was there. With paper in hand, I went back to the kitchen, made a steaming-hot cup of coffee and walked back upstairs to get ready for work.

Deciding last night that I was going to dress in conservative, comfortable, and practical attire for my first day at the office here, I took out my black, navy training hand-polished shoes, black slacks, matching black blazer and my light-yellow blouse. It was very similar to what I had worn back when I first reported to the Los Angeles Field Office, so I was confident that I looked professional.

"Thank you Lord," I said after my first cup of coffee was gone, my minimal make-up applied, and I was dressed.

I kissed Dave good-bye, who was up now, but still in his bathrobe because he had another day off.

"Let me drive you to the office," he said. "That way you won't get lost or be late on your first day."

"Its okay sweetie, I need to learn how to get around, so this is as good a day, as any to start. I'll be fine, but thanks for worrying about me, feels good to be worried about."

Twenty-five minutes later I arrived at the DFW CASFO, ten minutes early, and with plenty of unmarked parking spaces to choose from. I was relieved to be early, and very relieved to find so much parking. The parking lot at my old office was almost always full at any time of day or night.

Walking up to the second floor, I found the office. Only one or two lights were on in the building as I found my way upstairs to report for duty.

I was excited and nervous, the palms of my hands were sweating and my heart was beating like mad beneath my yellow blouse. *Calm down Maggie. Its goanna be okay.* I silently said a prayer.

Not only was it okay, it was perfect. I was met with an enormous amount of Texas hospitality, lots of handshakes, long conversations about where I was living, life in California, who my husband was, what I liked most about this job, on and on the conversations went. All my fears were dispelled within minutes. It was a marvelous welcome to Texas.

Agents shared offices here so I wasn't going to be sitting out in a big open room. And our two agent offices had a view of empty, wild-grass fields. It was lovely. The carpet was tan and brown, not bright orange and stained with coffee and other unidentifiable goo. I was a happy camper by the end of the day even though I missed working with Agent Stanton and Big Earl. Heck, I even missed Don a.k.a. "Big Bird" who was always trying to sabotage any logistics the FAMS had to do, simply because he was a want-to-be air marshal. We called him "Big Bird" because he was extremely tall, had a bulb of a nose, and had afro hair that was fuzzy and light, light brown. His hair color was so light it was almost blonde.

By week's end, I had a DFW Airport and Dallas Love Field Airport ID Badges. I was assigned American Airlines as my carrier at DFW

Airport and Randy Mitchell was my working partner like Agent Stanton was in Los Angeles.

The office manager, David Flowers, and supervisor Nelda Michaels, were really helpful in making sure my transfer orders were in place, that my pay was not be interrupted, and that I had all the tools I needed to perform my job.

David Flowers was a slim man, he looked like a runner, but he said he didn't run. "I don't run and I eat whatever I want too," he told me. He had brown eyes, a full head of hair, and wore wire rim glasses that sometime slid down his nose. He laughed a lot and had a open-door policy as long as you tried to resolve whatever issue you wanted to discuss with the supervisor first.

Supervisor Nelda Michaels was older than David, I think. She wasn't pretty- she was sort of plain-but she dressed to the nines: killer coordination from head to toe, matching shoes with every outfit, and she drove a yellow corvette. She was married, but I didn't know if she had any kids. She was smart and savvy without a doubt. She knew our aviation security manual like the back of her hand. She was a true professional, and I really admired her.

This office and management are really efficient. I thought to my-self. *I'm going to learn a lot here.*

The agent I shared an office with, Dale McCaulk, was a special agent who conducted physical security inspections along with some airport and airline inspections in Oklahoma. He was married, had no children, was very reserved, and he talked to his wife at least four times a day. I found out later that his wife was uncomfortable that he was sharing an office with a "girl agent" as I was referred to, so she called several times a day to check up on him.

Overall the transition from LAX CASFO to DFW CASFO was very smooth. My pay never stopped, my workload increased, along with my skill sets and abilities to adapt quickly to new environments. I loved it. I love the agents, the management team, and the work.

Along with a smooth work transition, I was making friends at home too. A few weeks after moving to Coppell, Dave and I went to the pool at our complex to go swimming. Summertime was in full swing and it was hotter than blazes. But neither of us minded since we were sun worshipers without a doubt. Our towels wrapped snugly around our waists, we walked hand in hand to the pool, with our flip flops slapping against the hot pavement.

Dave was flying out tomorrow for a two night over night in Puerto Rico, so after today, I'd be on my own for the first time since moving here just a few weeks ago.

As the gate clicked behind us, we went in search of two lounge chairs in a location with some shade, but mostly sun.

"Gosh, the water is getting so warm, Dave." I said as I slipped into the warm, clear pool.

"Yes, it's really, really nice. Only thing they need poolside here is a BBQ." Dave replied.

I nodded my head and then ducked under the water, pushed off from the side as I began swimming laps. I still had an excellent stroke from learning how to swim at an early age and being on several swim teams, including the United States Naval swim team. I loved the water, both salt and fresh.

I didn't swim as much now that I was an air marshal. Running was the sport of choice because I needed to time qualify twice a year in the mile and a half run. So, I slowly traded my fins for running shoes and took to the streets early in the morning before work or late in the afternoon when it was cooler. I wasn't use to having to worry about weather because in Southern California you could run almost any day of the year. But I was adapting to this change without too much trouble.

Dave and I heard the pool gate open before we saw who had come to join us at the pool. But soon enough we heard a hardy hello. Helen Hunter from unit S5 was walking through the gate with a pitcher full of lime daiquiri, a box of wheat thins, and cheese.

"Well, good golly, I was hoping someone would be here to help me drink this pitcher of liquid job." She said with a smile, a laugh, and a twinkle in her eye while handing us a plastic cup.

MEETING THE NEIGHBORS ⮡

"Oh darn, if we have too," I said as I climbed out of the pool.

The water evaporated as quickly off my body in the hot Texas sun as the three of us sipped our adult beverages. Helen excused herself as she went to make another batch.

Our complex had four buildings in it, and I'm not sure how many townhomes. Helen and Roger lived in the building across from the parking lot and one building over. They were closer to the pool than we were, and we were closer to the mail boxes than they were.

Dave and Helen met a few years ago when Dave went to lease a car. Helen was the sales person that helped him. They had become friends and stayed in contact through the years. She was the one that told Dave about the townhome we were renting.

I learned that Helen was about five years younger than I was and Roger was a few years older which were a lot like Dave and I, in that, Dave was 10 years older than me.

Helen and Roger were two of the funniest people I had ever met. Their humor was swift, quick-witted, and directed both at themselves and others. No harm, just plain fun. Within minutes after meeting them I felt right at home and I knew we'd be friends for a very long time.

Helen was a beauty, with curly black hair that touched the top of her shoulders, big black saucer eyes, a thin perfectly shaped nose, skinny legs, and a full figured bust-line that even Dolly Parton would be jealous of.

Roger was tall, 6'2", with thin, sandy-grey hair that he kept neat and trimmed short, but not military short. His nose was slightly out of proportion to his face, and sun burnt from too many years working outside in the Texas sun. He was a character too. Helen and Roger-a pair indeed.

"Yes indeed, we want good neighbors and fun neighbors. That's what we want around here," she told Dave.

And I have to admit, they were a blast: always a party, always good will, great food, and ever a better bar.

Helen and Roger weren't married and they didn't have any kids.

I'm not sure if they wanted kids since Roger had two from a previous marriage, but they had a couple of cats and a million friends to keep them company. Plus, they never forgot your name or your favorite beverage. And, Roger made hamburgers to die for.

"Want to come over for Big Daddy burgers later?" Helen asked.

I looked at Dave and he nodded his head in the affirmative, so I said, "Sure, what can we bring?"

"Bring whatever you want to drink and a jar of pickles if you have any, I'm out." She said.

"You got it." I said as I sipped my refreshingly tart lime daiquiri.

If you wanted a party, no matter the day of the week, show up at Helen and Rogers with a bottle of wine, beer, or spirits and the party would begin. Roger's favorite was Crown and Helen inexpensive white wine. Dave and I drank wine, and occasionally Dave would drink rum. We were definitely lite weights compared to the drinking skills of Helen and Roger.

A small party began that Wednesday evening. Once the BBQ was started and the aroma of Big Daddy burgers filled the air, the neighbors, Joy, Bruce, and Jan, joined in for the festivities.

When Dave and I stumbled home, just before midnight, I knew it was going to be a rough day at work tomorrow. Agent Randy Myers, my partner and I were meeting with the American Airlines Station Manager at 10 A.M. to discuss the findings and a few violations we had uncovered during our inspection of their facility over the past month. But Randy and I were meeting at the office at 7 A.M.

"Oh dear, I'm going to be a basket case tomorrow, Honey," I said as I crawled into bed.

"Well, if you're going to be a basket case, you might as well really be a basket case," Dave said with a mischievous smile.

"Oh, I know that look," I laughed and ducked under the covers.

"You can hide Missy, but you can't escape." Dave said as he dove after me.

We laughed, giggled, and made love.

"Yep, I'm going to be a mess tomorrow, Dear." I said as yawned wide mouthed and loudly. "Sorry Honey."

We kissed, rolled over on our sides, and closed our already bloodshot eyes to get some precious sleep.

Rough was an understatement when the alarm clock went off, but I dragged myself out of bed, got dress and headed for the office. I didn't look like the walking dead, but I felt close to it when I walked in the office at 7:00 A.M.

Randy and I were just about done comparing our agent notes, but we needed a few more hours to verify everything we wanted to discuss with American Airlines.

Personally, I was grateful to have a few extra hours in the office because meeting the neighbors was still swirling around inside my blood stream.

CHAPTER 10

Skies Over Texas

"Sweetie, it's time to leave. I've got to scoot or I'll be late." I hollered up to Dave who was still upstairs getting ready for his trip.

"Okay, I'll be right down, Dear." He hollered back.

Dave put his bag in the back of the VW we recently purchased. It was bright-bright orange and had a small dent on the rear, right bumper. Even with 90,000 miles it ran like a top and was really fun to drive. My first car was a VW Bug, so any member of the VW family brought back happy memories.

After dropping Dave off at the cargo facility on the east side of the airport, I cut across the south end and back around the golf course to get to the office. Fortunately, I was about five minutes ahead of Randy.

Whew, my luck. I thought as I smiled and looked out my office window. I looked down on my VW and let out a chuckle.

Oh, the hippie is still alive in you, huh girl? Even though you're a fed now. I chuckled out loud.

"What's so funny?" Are you laughing because I'm late….again?" Agent Mitchell asked when he walked into my office.

"Nah, I'm just laughing about my car that's all. What's wrong with you, you look like you got shot through canon?" I said with a slight tone of concern in my voice.

"Oh, I had a flat on the way in. No biggie, just a pain in the butt to fix is all. Damn potholes get me every time." He said with his normally cheery attitude.

"Well I'm glad it's only that. Guess we should finish up this report before we head out." I said while opening my black binder with the large Federal Aviation Administration, Aviation Security logo embossed on the front.

The office bought every agent one with some of their end of year funding. It wasn't a normal purchase, but binders were very handy to have, good quality and attractive.

Randy and I spent about an hour finalizing our notes before we grabbed a G-car and headed for the American Airlines Offices located in Terminal A. It was a short ride, made even shorter with the transmitters we had that allowed us access into restricted areas of the airfield.

"I'm glad we have the transponder on this car," I said to Randy. "It probably saves us ten minutes in drive time and parking hassles. Sometimes being a fed has its perks."

We parked our car in the designated spot for government vehicles and made our way to the American Airlines Station Managers Office located on the third floor. Unlike, the American Airlines office that I visited often while working at Ontario Airport in California, this office space was enormous, had plush furnishings, and a view of the airport that had to be the envy of any airline station manager based at DFW.

You could see as far as the eye could see. Big skies that looked like the color of the deep, blue ocean: crystal clear and calm. The view of the enormous runways stretching across wide open spaces, with their flickering lights, was mesmerizing. Off in the distance, you could see the fenced-off fields waiting for additional airport expansion. Growth that would ultimately happen because DFW was the largest airport in the United States based on the number of acres it sat on.

"Randy, I swear everything is bigger in Texas."

"It is!" Randy said like a true Texan.

Our meeting lasted an hour, and once it was finished Randy and I walked through the adjoining American Airlines Terminals.

"Everyone is so gracious." I said to Randy as we headed for Terminal B.

"Yep, that's Texas style. No matter if they get dinged and are madder than hell, they'll be gracious to your face and curse about you later over a beer or scotch." Randy said.

"Well, God Bless Texas." I said.

Randy looked at the ground a few feet in front of him, just about the same time I did. We both scrambled to pick up the five dollar bill we saw laying on the ground. Randy got to it first, scooping it up with his right hand, closing his fingers firmly over the paper money.

"I'll split it with you, I promise," he said with a loud hoot and a holler as we both stepped onto the people walker that would transport us between Terminal A and B.

"Works for me," I said.

"Let's go get ice cream," Randy said.

"Well, that works for me too." I said.

We were so preoccupied with finding money that we didn't see the end of the people mover quickly approaching. We both stumbled, almost tumbling into a heap on the floor. Somehow we managed not to fall, but it took every bit of balance, arms failing frantically in the air, like birds trying to take flight after being startled.

It must have looked comical, and we laughed until we almost cried once we regained our composure and began walking through the terminal in search of ice cream. We celebrated our airline assessment closure with a waffled-coned Rocky Road ice cream.

"Yep, two special agents stumbled and created havoc at the American Airlines terminal today, all for five dollars."

"Too, too funny Randy, and I hope no one we know saw us." I said.

"Me too," Randy said with a big grin and just a little chocolate smudged on the corners of his mouth.

When we arrived back at the CASFO, I had a note on my chair to stop by Supervisor Nelda's desk.

Well, I wonder what this is about. I thought as I picked up the note from my chair and placed it on my desk.

I tapped on Nelda's door and waited to be called into her office. She had a corner office with an incredible view looking to the south. Her office was small in comparison to the manager's office, but the view was ten times better.

"Hi, come on in Maggie." She said once she turned around from her computer.

"How was your exit briefing today with American?" she asked.

"I think it went well. Randy and I tagged teamed the briefing with each of us talking about the various findings and violations we discovered. It seemed to make sense since we were, in essence, the subject matter experts for our own data collection." I replied.

"Good Maggie, sounds like it went well then. Now, the reason I called you into my office is because you've been selected for random drug testing. I'm not sure if you were ever selected in L.A. or not." she said.

"No, I know as agents were subject to testing, but I've never been drug tested since I was hired." I said.

Supervisor Nelda began explaining since special agents held top secret security clearances and we were in sensitive positions, it was mandatory, that unannounced drug and alcohol testing be given.

"And Maggie, it's your lucky day because you need to go to the Regional Office, report to medical, and following their instructions to the tee," she said. "Oh, and take this paper with you. Go now; do not go anywhere else between here and the regional office."

"And by-the-way Maggie, I don't know who's going to be tested. Medical calls me on the phone and they tell me specifically who they want to see. No choice, no escaping since it's a mandatory. It's one of the perks for having a security clearance."

"Okay, I'll go now. I hope Rocky Road ice cream isn't a trigger," I said with a devilish grin.

"I'll see you tomorrow. Make sure you bring the G-car back here to-night. I can't authorize you to take it home, but I can authorize overtime since I know you'll be there longer than 2:30 P.M. when you're suppose to go home."

"Okay, I'll take the OT. Thanks, and see you tomorrow," I said as I walked out of the office.

I grabbed a set of keys from the lock box that was located in the stor-age area in our office building. I signed the log, stopped by my office to grab my briefcase, and to tell my partner where I was going. With my briefcase and paperwork in hand I finally headed for the parking lot.

When I opened the car door it must have been well over a hundred inside. The heat rushed out at me like a storm trying to escape captivity in search of freedom.

I left the car door open while I did a quick walk around to make sure the car didn't have any major dents or flat tires. While doing my pre-flight check, so-to-speak, my mind drifted back to Agent Stanton and his extreme for dirty G-cars.

He always said, "If you want to look professional, than everything about you needs to look professional, including the car you drive. Remember when you're a federal employee – aka 'fed' – everyone has their eye on you everywhere you go. When you drive or walk around airports, airlines, cargo facilities, and even driving to lunch, you are be-ing observed. Don't forget that."

And here I was about to drive 25 miles to the regional office in a very fifthly G-car.

Agent Stanton wouldn't like the condition of this car at all.

As I pulled out of the parking lot I made a mental note to call Stanton. After leaving Los Angeles, we hadn't talked enough. I missed him and Big Earl.

The Southwest Regional Office was just off Interstate 35W, and it was about a twenty-five minute drive from the office across various freeways that took me through the cities of Euless, Hurst, and Bedford before arriving just on the outskirts of Ft. Worth.

The single story, depilated, white building sat on a gigantic piece of land as well, separated from other buildings by a barb-wire fence. I was told it was once a glue factory-in killing horses to make glue, type factory-so it gave me the creeps every time I went near the place.

I wondered why on earth the government would select this building, and this location, of all places to have their Southwest Regional Office. Plus this place is so far away from the airport.

The staff that worked here had geographical responsibility for airports and their airlines within the state of Texas, Oklahoma, New Mexico, Louisiana, and Arkansas. This region's geographical area was huge, coupled with the fact that American Airlines had a major hub here.

I bet every visit made by any airport or airline official had them shaking their head when they left the FAA's Corporate Offices.

Well, this place is one testament of tax payer dollars NOT being spent. I mumbled as I walked into the depilated building.

In the medical office I completed the required paperwork, was escorted by a nurse to the ladies restroom next door, and I peed into a container that was sealed and hand delivered back to the nurse, who stood just outside my stall door while I peed.

After completing the drug testing I was told I could return to my office.

The process was very straight forward and, yes, it was an inconvenience to drive twenty-five miles, but now I was getting paid overtime since my eight hour shift had just ended.

Once again, welcome to federal service. Sometimes it's best to go with the flow, not ask questions, and move onto the next day. I love this job so it's worth it. I said once my G-car door slammed closed and once again I was heading back to the CASFO.

To my surprise, when I got back to the office at 430 P.M., my supervisor was still there.

"Hi, you're still here." I said while hanging the G-car keys back up and signing the log book.

"I'm just finishing up some last minute paperwork," she said.

"Looks like you and a few of your fellow agents are leaving on a mission next week. As always, bad timing for the office, but we'll manage."

"Great, where are we going?" I excitedly asked.

"You're off to Egypt, Israel, and a few places in-between. Now that should be an interesting trip. Wish I wasn't in management, I'd love to go too."

"So get going, get home, you'll have a full plate for the next couple of weeks before you head out," she said.

"Okay, I'm heading out now. See you tomorrow."

On the drive home, I was ecstatic. I hadn't been on a mission for almost six months. I was ready to travel again, hopefully see some of my colleagues from the West Coast, and contribute to protecting our country. I always had a profound sense of patriotism when I flew on Air Marshal Missions.

"Yes!" I said as I slapped my hand on the steering wheel.

On the other hand, when I got home, Dave was not as excited as I was when I told him about the mission that would take me away from home for almost three weeks.

"I wish you didn't have to go Maggie," Dave said during dinner that evening. "I'll miss you."

"'I'll miss you too. But being gone comes with this job," I said as I reached my left hand across the table and touched his forearm.

Dave looked across the table at me; giving me a half-hearted smile, of which I clearly understood by his facial expressions that he, was not at all happy that I was heading out for a mission.

I had a hunch that trouble was storming, not only over the skies of Texas tonight, but trouble was already brewing in Dave's mind too.

Well this isn't good. I thought while getting up from the table to clear the dishes. *He knew I'd be traveling eventually with this job, but he sure seems upset now.*

CHAPTER 11

Did You Say Camel?

Water? Is it all really about water, oil, natural gas, and religion? The classified briefing we just sat through lasted more than two hours. Our team looked antsy to get out of the tiny, cramped conference room we had all been stuffed into for this briefing.

I received my orders about ten days ago to report to Washington, D.C., for my first trip to Egypt and Israel. The two countries had been fighting for hundreds of years. In 1978 the two countries signed a peace treaty that terminated the war between them and created the withdrawal of both armed forces and civilians from the Sinai, behind the international boundary between Israel and Egypt. The treaty opened the international waterways, including the Suez Canal, the Striates of Tiran and Eilat as well.

Nevertheless, the relationship between the two countries was sometimes described as a "cold peace" with many citizens in both countries skeptical about their future.

Pushing through the revolving door at the Holiday Inn on SW 9th Street, I felt comfortable. Comfortable because I was very familiar with it since I always tried to stay here when I came to Washington. As I dragged my bag behind me, feeling its weight, after the flight from Dallas I was exhausted. Plus, the middle seat I had sat in for three hours only added to my fatigue. Hearing the tiny suitcase wheels clacking along on the flooring behind me was a constant reminder that I was on the road.

The last time I was in Washington, D.C., I was giving a briefing to Director Sword, Agent Quinn, and a variety of other security types who wanted to hear all about the unfortunate death of Special Agent Brown, which had happened while we were traveling together in Stockholm.

When we were traveling together Agent Brown suffered a brain aneurysm during our taxi ride to the hotel. After being on life support for a week, with no change, the hospital informed me that his physician had recommended he be taken off life support. It was a tragic event, a first for FAA Security, so the aftermath briefings were intense, but necessary.

I recall saying, "Common sense, for the most part, was the first thing I did. I was alone, I knew I needed help, I was in a foreign country, so to me, it was logical that I contact the US Embassy for assistance." And that's what I had done.

After that trip Maggie Stewart was a common household name throughout FAA Security. And this notoriety made me have to repeat this sad story again and again.

Once at the hotel desk, I checked in, and then went to my room. I dropped my bag, changed into my running clothes, and headed out the hotel door in a westerly direction towards the L'Enfant Plaza Metro Station. I passed the Federal Aviation Headquarters Building on 7th Street S.W. and Independence, and found "The Mall" one block to the north. I needed a good long run after being crammed between two very large men, both managing to horde the arm rests for the entire flight.

I ran on the hard packed dirt that stretched for a mile. It was an uncomplicated run, one mile up, and then back, the strip of grass dividing the paths. I felt my patriotism building in me as quickly as a hawk spies and falls upon it's pray.

"I love America," I said as each step carried me closer and closer to the Washington Memorial at the West end of The Mall. I ran two miles in the warm evening air, passing by the Smithsonian, then the Natural History Museum, and finally the Capitol. It was an amazing run.

When I got back to my room, I was starving, so I quickly cleaned up, and went downstairs to find some dinner.

I easily found my way to the office the next morning. I rode the elevator to the third floor and stepped off the elevator to find Agent Stanton, Big Earl, and an agent I didn't know standing in the hallway. They were trying to figure out where to go.

"Good morning guys. See that green tile among the shiny gray military-style ones? Turn in that direction and you'll always find our offices-double doors-at the end of the hallway." I said with a laugh.

"Well, aren't you the smart one." Agent Bridge said with a smirk.

"Yes, I am. Hi I'm Maggie Stewart." I said while extending my hand.

"Hi, I'm Jill Bridge."

The four of us walked down the hallway looking for the ACS Office. We were ready to get going and hear what our assignment entailed.

We signed in and were escorted to the secure skiff. Agent Matt Kelsey of the Office on Intelligence introduced himself.

"Good afternoon. I hope all of you had a pleasant journey here from your home offices. It's a bit unusual to conduct these security briefings here in headquarters, but the Dulles CASFO is begin remodeled so it made sense to come here instead." He said.

"As you know, you're heading to Cairo, Egypt, and Israel tomorrow afternoon. Your flight and hotel information is contained in the packets I'll hand to you shortly.

"The specificity of the threat creating the need for this mission is the ongoing tension in the Middle East towards U.S. entities. Egypt and Israel have had strained relations between the two countries, even though they signed a Peace Treaty in 1978."

"Any questions so far?" Matt asked.

"Okay then," he continued. "You'll be flying under the cover of two passports. Please use your brown official passport when traveling to Egypt and use your blue personal passport when traveling to and from Israel. We do not want either country to know that you have been traveling elsewhere. Is that clear?"

Everyone in the room either quietly said yes or nodded their head, letting Matt know that they understood what was required of them.

"Good, now let's get down to some specific threat information." Matt continued.

When we left the "skiff" two hours later, our heads were full of information that was valuable for understanding why we were traveling to this part of the world for work. Along with the security briefing we had other bits and pieces of information regarding safety tips and specific locations that we were not allowed to travel to, sadly, one of which was the City of Jerusalem.

"Americans, at least you ladies and gentlemen, cannot visit the city." Matt said with a particularly strong emphasis on "cannot".

"Darn, I know Jerusalem is a center of pilgrimage for Christians, like me, Jews, and Muslims. I was hoping to see that scared city."

At 5 P.M., when the briefing was finished, I walked down the hall to see if I could find anyone I knew. But most of the cubical and office spaces were vacated.

"Washingtonians are very punctual when it comes to making their train or metro rides," I said to no one in particular as I left the building and walked back to my hotel.

After another short run, and a quick meal, I called home. When no one answered the phone, I remembered that Dave had left for a four-day trip this morning.

Darn, now I won't talk to him for a few days, I quietly thought. *Guess it's time to call it a day.*

The team was facing a grueling eleven hour and thirty-seven minute flight to Cairo tomorrow and I wanted as much sleep as I could.

"Night Lord," I said as I switched off the table lamp beside the bed and curled up in a ball so I could, hopefully, sleep the night away.

The following morning, the short flight from Washington, D.C., to John F. Kennedy in New York felt more like a bus ride than an airline flight. The plane was loud, compact, and bumpy. The team was connecting with a United Airlines B-747 that we would be flying on to Egypt's International Airport in Cairo.

I always marveled at the difference in how people acted in one airport to another. At Dulles, everyone was in a hurry, news papers tucked underneath their arms or stuffed in the back of their roller bags as they scurried through the airport. There was no time for eye contact, no time for chit-chat, just time to rush, rush, rushing away their lives feeling important.

John F. Kennedy, JFK as we called it was so different. People were still in a tremendous rush, but they pushed, poked, and prodded their way along. And, they hollered along with their insistent invasion of any personal space you thought you might be entitled too. This type of crowd chaos could make you rattlesnake mad if you didn't control your temper.

I for one, by now, had gotten use to being shoved around at airports and having to fend for one's self, so I had a good time when I occasionally reciprocated with a gently nudge as I moved through the lines at the ticket counter and screening.

"No harm, no foul, just life at JFK," I said to Agent Stanton as we continued our long way in line.

"Yep, sometimes I wished we'd forget about this blending in with the public and just go onboard the damn aircraft."

"Whoa, sounds like you need a vacation my friend. What's up?" I asked.

"Just tired. And I am ready to do something else. I'm getting tired of being away from home and eating airplane food. Did you hear I bid on the supervisor's job at LAX? Drake's at the regional office now, so there's a vacancy at the CASFO. Interviewed last week, just waiting to hear now." He said.

"Well, well, that's big news. I hope you get it." I said as I patted him on the shoulder and bowed slightly.

"I'm in the presence of future management-wow." I said with a laugh.

After the team checked in, the lead agent for United Airlines escorted us behind the ticket counter and we walked, what seemed like a mile, before we reached a dirty, dingy, fingerprint covered door that lead us ramp-side.

Inside my head I thought, *I swear every airport looks the same once you get into the bowels of it.*

When the door leading to the ramp cracked open, you could hear the heartbeat of the airport immediately. Jet engines whined, tugs honked as they chugged along, and air operations van sped by with their lights flashing on the dome of their roofs. Flashing, as if, that would get them to their destination any faster. You could hear people hollering at one another so their voices could be heard above the vital and marvelous noise.

"I'll probably be deaf someday," I said, "but, golly, I'm going to be a very happy deaf woman."

Agent Stanton looked at me like I was crazy.

"I know, I know, but I love airports!"

We boarded prior to the passengers, conducted our aircraft security check, and were in our designated seats before the first class boarding began. As I took my seat in the economy section I put my backpack under the seat in front of me. I pushed it all the way forward in hopes that I'd have some leg room too.

My backpack was stuffed with my usual bounty of paper-back books that I brought at a used book store before each mission. Once read, I left it in the seat back pocket for the next passenger or cleaning crew to find. During each trip I read around ten books so buying used books was the best option for my budget.

As the passengers began boarding, I felt my mind changes gears so I could carefully watch and observe them as they rambled down the aisles looking for their assigned seats. Once everyone was on-board every seat had been taken.

Yep, we're in for a long flight Maggie. I thought as I looked at the couple seated at the window and middle seats.

The woman next to me was short and round, in fact, almost entirely round. She managed to squeeze herself into the seat, but I wasn't sure she'd be able to get out at the end of the flight.

The man next to her, who I presume was her husband, spoke with an exceptionally deep voice and his eyes were full of curiosity and awareness. His cotton, button-down shirt had one coffee stain on it and two pens clipped onto the shirt's pocket. His thick, horn-rim glasses made me think he was a professor of some type and this was their adventure of a lifetime.

They held hands as the flight attendants performed the security briefings, checked that everyone's seatbelts were fastened, and tray tables closed and stowed.

"Here we go, Maggie. Here we go, again." I whispered as we lifted into the bumpy East Coast skies.

By the time we landed in Cairo, I knew Fred and Margaret were newlyweds who had met at the University of New York where they both taught. Margaret taught English literature and Fred taught economics. They both had a keen interest in seeing the pyramids so, for their honeymoon; they were spending two weeks traveling to see as many pyramids as they could. They were a cute couple: smart, content, and totally at peace with life.

When I told them to have fun and go in peace, they responded with smiles and said, "Thanks and stay in peace, for you look very happy and content."

Tears welled up in my eyes; I smiled and thought *yes, I am very content indeed.*

"What a mad house," I shouted to Big Earl as we shoved our way towards the main doors of the terminal while we pulled our bags firmly along behind us.

"The pushing and shoving around here is just like New York, but I can't understand a word anyone is saying," I shouted again.

"Welcome to Cairo, Maggie. You'll adapt!" Big Earl said with a grin.

"Look guys," Agent Joe G. yelled as we were just about to exit the terminal in search for cabs. He then licked the terminal wall with his pink, pointy tongue!

"Ew," I shouted in disgust. "Are you for real?" I couldn't believe my eyes.

"I guarantee if you do that, you won't ever get sick in any country you travel too," Joe said with complete conviction. "Come on, try it Maggie, I dare you."

"Not a chance in hell Joe will you find me licking an airport terminal wall, in any airport. As a matter-of-fact any wall for that matter." I said as I backed away. "Get away from me."

The rest of the team just laughed. "Yep Joe G. is a crazy son-of-a-bitch." remarked Agent Stanton.

The heat hit us first with a blast of dry, hot, arid, scorching desert heat that felt like we had stepped under a blazing heat lamp. Then the blazing sun light momentarily blinded all of us, as we either shielded our eyes or quickly put on our sunglasses.

Tucked inside the spacious black and white checkered cabs, we rode mostly in silence to the Intercontinental Cairo Semiramis Hotel that was about 15 miles from the airport.

While looking outside the window, I saw drab, dusty buildings, tall mosques, and people in cars, cabs, buses, motor scooters, and on foot.

Silly as it sounded, for the first time in my many travels, I felt like I was in a foreign country; the sights and smells made me uneasy. I had a feeling of not being totally safe. Those feelings kept me on edge from the instant I stepped outside Terminal Two and into the noisy, crowded, traffic-riddle sidewalk.

I'm not sure about this place. Wish I had my firearm tucked inside my backpack, was all I could think of at that particular moment.

As we piled out of the cabs in front of the hotel we were met by hotel employees who were more than willing to assist us with our bags. I had a firm rule to always hang onto my personal luggage, so I smiled and said, "No thank you".

The Intercontinental Hotel was less than ten years old, build in 1987 with 28 floors and 735 rooms to choose from. It was situated very close to the Nile on Conniche El Nil Street. It was gorgeous inside and had beautiful seating for guests in the lobby, mirrors, chandeliers, and expensive lamps adorning the fine wood tables. The comparison to the streets and buildings outside was in stark contrast to one another.

Maybe I should stay in this trip" I thought. *Nah, I've got to go see the Egyptian pyramids at least. Come on; don't let this place spook you.*

After checking in, we all met in the team leader's room on the fifteenth floor to debrief. Agent Lopez had command of this team once again so the briefing was quick, efficient, and to the point. After we submitted our time sheets we were free to go.

Tomorrow would be a down day for the team so Agent Stanton, Big Earl and I made arrangements to meet in the lobby the next morning to go and tour the nearby pyramids in the City of Giza.

The following morning the three of us met the driver who would be guiding us for the day to and from the pyramids. We met at the conceigiers desk.

"Good morning," he said as he greeted us with a warm, friendly smile. "Your driver today is Razi, who is an excellent guide. All of your expenses will be billed to your hotel rooms, so the only money you'll need is for a tip that you may want to give to Razi. Your tour will last most of the day."

"Sounds fine," Big Earl said. "We are looking forward to seeing the pyramids and riding a camel perhaps."

"I didn't volunteer to get on a camel," I chimed in.

"Maggie, Maggie, trust me, it will be all right," Big Earl said with an enormous grin.

The thirty-minute drive from the hotel to the City of Giza was met with wide-eyed anticipation on my part. As I watched women shrouded from head to toe go about their daily business, men smoking and chattering about who-knows-what and drab buildings with coverings over each and every window, I felt like I was being watched from those tiny darkened window frames.

As we drove along Pyramids Road, I was also shocked to see a tip of one pyramid rising above the famous golden arches of a McDonalds.

"Well, well, will you look at that." Agent Stanton said.

Arriving at the world-famous, pyramids of Giza, I saw hordes of tourist and knew we'd blend right in. Our cab driver, now our guide, took us to a ticket booth that was very close to the Sphinx in the eastern section of the plateau.

"This area is called the Giza Plateau and at one time, not too long ago, was only open, barren desert. But the sprawl of civilization and tourism in the past twenty years have turned this area into a compound almost, but at least our precious pyramids are safe," our guide said.

"Come, let me show you around," as we waved his hand for us to follow him.

"Our first stop is the Temple of the Sphinx which is a colossal, recumbent human-headed lion. We call it the "Father of Terror."

"It's smaller than I thought it would be," I said to everyone.

"Yes, it's the smallest pyramid here, but it's different in that it was carved from a single giant block of Sandstone." Our guide said in impeccable English.

"What happened to its nose?" asked Big Earl.

"We believe the missing nose is from target practice by some very bored British soldiers during World War I or perhaps from the Turks in the late 1700's. Either way it is very sad."

"Yes, it is. It's beautiful. Will you take our picture?" I asked.

"Yes, yes of course," our guide happily said as we all lined up to have our picture taken. I normally don't take pictures, especially with fellow team members but this was just about impossible to resist.

Wait till Dave see's this. He'll love it. I thought.

"Care to go inside one of our pyramids?" Our guide asked.

"Absolutely," Big Earl barked.

"Before we venture into the pyramids can we stop at the rest-room first?" I asked our guide.

"Yes, yes of course. Right this way."

After spending the better part of the morning seeing the Great Sphinx, the Pyramid of Khafre, and the interior of the Khufu Pyramid, our day of touring was complete except for a camel ride.

Lining up with a few other tourists, I could tell that this was going to be an experience of a lifetime. "Good or bad, this is going to be interesting guys," I said as we took under the hot sun, fanning ourselves with the guide booklets we were given at the beginning of our tour.

Climbing up into the saddle was a feat in itself. My cantankerous camel did not want one more tourist riding on its back. The noise and spit was unbelievable as the handler tried to get the camel to move forward to give me a ride along the prearranged dirt path. But the camel was clearly not cooperating, my ride, I suspect, was shorter than anticipated, well by everyone but the camel. Climbing off the camel I was greeted with shouts and cheers from our tour guide and I managed to have one picture taken beside this brown beast.

After our smell, noisy, spitting, fortunately short-lived camel ride, the drive back to the hotel was extremely peaceful and cool for the cabs' air conditioning was running full blast by then.

We bid farewell, generously tipped our guide, and walked back into the hotel. It was a long, yet very interesting day, full of rich surroundings, history, and a short but unforgettable camel ride. I was ready to find a hot meal and a warm bed. Tomorrow morning at 7 A.M., we'd be on our way again, this time to Israel in a roundabout way.

CHAPTER 12

Superior Weapons

As we lifted off and sped away from Cairo, I let out a huge sigh of relief. It felt good to be airborne again.

I had tried to calling home several times from my hotel room and hadn't been able to get through. I was melancholy. I missed my husband.

The only souvenir I was taking from Egypt was a cartouche with my name inscribed on it and a few photos in my camera. Everything else, the grime of the city, the veiled women, and shuttered windows, I wanted to leave behind, well, except the memories of visiting the City of Giza and the marvelous pyramids.

My cartouche was a required purchase, at least as described by my fellow team mates. Once you wore a cartouche, or "FAM Dog Tag," around your neck, you were a true FAM. How this tradition got started I'll never know but at least I had saved enough per diem money to buy one. And a beautiful 18-carat gold rope chain to hang it on. Tucked safely in my backpack, nestled among spare pair socks and underwear, it was safe for the ride home.

After eight hours of flying we landed in Paris. Watching the passengers deplane, we all began to relax knowing that another leg of our mission was complete. Soon we'd be meeting with law enforcement officials to check our firearms into their country. We'd stay one night and depart for Israel tomorrow.

Paris was always an interesting place to visit: the Eiffel Tower, the Louvers, Sacred Heart Cathedral, just to name a few, were spectacular to visit. But sadly, the French weren't very gracious towards Americans. I guess they forgot that they gave us the Statue of Liberty as a gesture of friendship and a testament to our democracy since they were struggling with their own government at the time. Today, the relationship between American and France is rocky. Rocky like the storm the ship endured as it set sail to the United States, in 1886, carrying 210 crates representing light, liberty, and justice. That storm nearly capsized the ship. I could feel a storm between these two countries brewing, one that I hoped would capsize the two countries relations any further.

After flying multiple times into and out of this country, I was use to their sullen attitude towards us. I no longer took it personally; I myself became more demanding, just to spite people's surly attitudes. It was kind of a vicious circle, but somehow it was the logical way to be.

In my hotel room, I plopped my bag on my bed, quickly changed, and headed out for a short run before dinner.

Eating dinner at 9 P.M. is always a struggle for me, because I was always hungry hours earlier. But I had learned to pack a few dry snacks in my backpack so I'd have some fuel to hold me over.

As I yawned, my mouth hanging open, I said, "Ok, let's get outside and say hello to Paris."

Running along the streets while dodging the occasion pile of feces inadvertently left by a Parisian dog owner my mind wondered to another city, another country, and one that was so very different from where I was tonight.

I miss Coppell, my husband, our townhome, and our friends. But I was excited about tomorrow.

Tomorrow I was about to go to going to Israel, the birth place of Christ. I was really excited knowing that I was going to see some of the surrounding areas on the outskirts of Tel Aviv. Sadly, we couldn't go into Jerusalem; the city was off limits, due to the current animosity, and threat level towards Americans. But we could travel north from Tel Aviv to wander around the Jordan River, the Sea of Galilee, and other sacred places.

I'm ready, I said as I kicked up my pace.

I can't remember any time that our entire team met for dinner, but tonight even Agent Lopez joined in on the festivities. Inside the restaurant, the walls looked like they were made of large, round, tan river rocks. I ran my hand over their smooth texture as we were taken to a table which was tucked away in the corner.

We dined on escargots, broiled meat, onions, green fresh vegetables and copious amounts of red table wine. The thick French bread was delicious and we all feasted until we were stuffed.

"I think they are going to have to reconfigure the weight and balance on the flight tomorrow," I said to Agent Rusty who was sitting next to me.

"I reckon they will," he said in his deep southern drawl.

"Anybody up for a walk to the Eiffel Tower?" Agent Bridge asked loudly, her speech slurred and voice shrill.

"She's indulged in too much wine," I said, "Sure hope we don't have to carry her butt home."

"Nah, we'll leave her sorry ass here if it comes to it." Agent Rusty said. "I think she's a royal pain."

"Hey, I heard that," And the piece of French bread she threw hit Agent Rusty square on the nose. "Just so you know, I think you're a pain too."

"I'm not putting up with you tonight," and Agent Rusty hurled a piece of bread at her.

Suddenly the entire table erupted and baskets of bread were emptied as the highly trained federal air marshals took aim at one another and began lobbing bread as if the accuracy of their aims were of utmost importance.

"Go, go, you must leave immediately," shouted the waiter who had seen this epic battle of bread begin from across the room. "Pay and go, you are no longer welcome here."

We tumbled out the door laughing, but soon the fresh evening air put a new perspective on our ill manners and we felt sheepishly ashamed as we walked, rather waddled down the street. We must have looked like a flock of Eider Ducks trying to find a nest as we waddled towards the Eiffel Tower.

The Eiffel Tower met us with her silent, majestic, and mechanical beauty. It stood towering over us: 10,000 feet tall, assembled with over 18,000 pieces and 2.5 million rivets.

"This was the world's fair exposition entrance," he said. Big Earl informed us that it had been build for the 1889 World's Fair and to mark the 100th anniversary year of the French Revolution. It took more than 2 years to build and was the tallest structure in France, in fact, the world for many, many years.

After riding the elevator to the top, we stood watching the sparkling Paris lights glimmer and shine around us. The sight was spectacular, but we knew it was time to end our tour and head back to the hotel. Daylight would be upon us before we knew it.

And, indeed, the morning dawn came with lightening speed, but I didn't mind for I was looking forward to seeing Israel.

After landing in Israel our team leader said, "Remember, brown passports here guys," as we gathered in the first class section prior to deplaning.

"Got it," Agent Stanton said in a loud voice ensuring that everyone heard him.

Digging my passport out of the zipped pouch of my navy blue backpack, I stood ready and waiting to get off this bird.

It's time to touch soil once again, I whispered to myself.

After landing, deplaning, and walking towards the first security checkpoint at the Tel Aviv Arrival area to begin our immigration and customs process, the same process that every passenger endured, I watched the back of Agent Lopez, Agent Stanton, and Big Earl heads as they waited in line. No one spoke a word; everyone nudged forward while quietly waiting to face the stern-faced agents that were visible up ahead.

Sometimes I really did wonder what the logic of the federal government was. I understood why we carried different passports to use while traveling to Israel and then into Arab countries: so the entry stamps did not appear in the same passport. But what I didn't understand is why we didn't request stamps that did not appear on our passport, an accommodation for other travelers, but we elected not to use.

Just don't lose your passports, Maggie, and you won't have to worry so much.

"Boker Tov." Big Earl said to the female agent as he handed her is passport.

She smile and replied "Good day" in English.

Dang, how does he know so many languages?

Silently watching and waiting for my turn in line, I saw that there were two lines snaking their way to the first security point where the mostly female, highly trained army graduates asked a specific series of questions to each arriving passenger as they presented their passports.

Each passport had to be valid at least six months from the date of their departure in order to gain entry into Israel. There were additional entry forms that needed to be completed with their personal details as well.

The lines moved quickly and once we cleared the first security checkpoint, we walked to the baggage claim area to get our luggage and proceed to the customs control area.

We didn't need entry visas, just our passports and entry form. Again, we were asked a few questions about our reason for visiting their country by these incredibly astute agents.

As we cleared customs one by one, we slowly gathered as a team in order to meet law enforcement officials to surrender our weapons while we were in country. This was customary in every country that we visited and, for the most part, every country had very similar chain of custody control procedures.

"Who is the team lead?" asked the Israeli officer on duty.

"I am." Agent Lopez said as the two shook hands.

"Pass these forms to your team, fill them out, keep the yellow copy, wrap the white copy around your firearm, make sure your gun is empty, and then place them in the box on the table here." He said in perfect English.

"We'll put them in our safe here at the airport and when you return on Wednesday make sure to have the yellow copy. It's very simple; we'll exchange one yellow copy for your firearm. Understand?" He said.

Agent Lopez nodded affirming that he understood and within about 15 minutes we had surrendered our firearms to the Israeli Security Forces and were on our way, looking for the exit.

As we walked through the terminal we saw several fit young men with duffle bags scattered throughout the airport, either standing with their bag at their feet, or they were walking through the terminal with purpose and determination in each step they took.

"I know who those guys are." Agent Stanton said.

"Yep, wish we could carry submachine guns at home." Big Earl replied. "That's a surefire way to keep the terrorist at bay. Bigger fire power and more visibility."

"What are they carrying?"

"I suspect Micro-Uzi's. They're smaller than the Parabellum Mimi-Uzi that was popular in the 1980's. These newer Uzi's were built for covert operations so the weapon could be easily concealed and deployed," Big Earl said, "But the Micro-Uzi has a really effective rate of fire and accuracy along with her sleek compact size."

"Do the airborne crews carry these as personal defense weapons too?" I asked.

"Yep, they sure do. Wait until we leave, Maggie."Big Earl smiled, "they're not so covert onboard either!"

Big Earl, what a guy I thought, not only does he know multiple languages but he know the Israeli air marshal's arsenal of weapons too. I bet the conversations at home with his wife Edith are pretty interesting since she's a fed too.

As our team exited the airport, we were immediately dumped into a sea of noise, people, taxis, and the general chaos that occurs outside every airport around the world. The only difference being, the visible level of security.

The twelve-mile ride to the hotel was quick but expensive. The fare was right around forty U.S. dollars.

"Whose turn is it to pay the cab fare?" Agent Stanton asked.

"I think I drew the short straw." I said as I opened my wallet and handed the money to Big Earl who was sitting up front. "Yikes, this city is expensive already."

CHAPTER 13

Land Of Inspirations

The Sheraton Tel Aviv Hotel proved to be modern and gorgeous. The high rise was right on the Mediterranean Sea and the view was spectacular.

"Almost every room in the hotel has a view of the sea, Miss Stewart," the handsome employee told me. "May I have your passport please?"

Handing him my passport, I looked around the hotel lobby briefly-scanning, along with taking in the beauty of this crisp, clean, and bright surroundings. The furniture was modern, lovely, and the fabric came in various shades of white or tan. The pictures were soothing seascapes.

"When was this hotel build?"

"This hotel was built in 1961 and it was the first Sheraton in the Middle East. We remodeled last year, and we feel this is the best hotel in all of Tel Aviv. You were very wise to choose us, and it is our pleasure that you are our guest."

"Thank you," I said as I collected my room key and went in search of the elevator that would take me to my room on the fourteenth floor.

The following morning I was ready to become a tourist. I had been anxiously awaiting this adventure to explore this fascinating country for years.

When I stepped off the elevator, almost dancing, I saw Agent Stanton, Big Earl, and Agent Jill Bridge sitting in the lobby. I was fifteen minutes early-so were they-which told me they were looking forward to our day of exploring as much as I was.

"Morning,"

"Morning, Maggie!" Everyone chimed in unison.

Walking out the hotel into the bright morning sun, I stepped alongside Agent Bridge. I hadn't spent any time with her on this mission and now I was curious to get to know her better, especially after she created last night's expulsion from the restaurant where were dining. I wondered why she always seemed so put off by everyone, including me. So I figured there was no better time than the present to find out. Plus, I had heard about the stunt Joe G. had played on her in Egypt one that almost put the two of them in jail.

Joe G. thought it would be "cute" to try and sell Jill to some Arabs who told him that they were interested in women from America. I had only heard this second hand, but somehow he had actually brokered a deal and was going to take Jill to them, as a practical joke. Thankfully, Agent Lopez got wind of the practical joke and squashed it before anyone actually met.

"We have some real jack-asses on this trip," Agent Lopez told us the next morning after the incident. "I should send his sorry ass home, but I can't jeopardize the overall mission at this point."

"This trip report will read like a novel by the time we're done." He said in utter disgust.

Jill seemed a little snobby when we first met in Washington, D.C., a few weeks ago, and I wondered if my first impression of her was right or wrong.

First impressions are usually accurate, but I felt compelled, since she was a part of our team, to give her another chance.

Come on Maggie, turn on the charm girl, I thought.

Agent Bridge was from the Seattle Field Office and had been with the FAA for about two years. She looked younger than me, no wedding ring, and her straight bleach blonde hair hung just below her shoulders. Her blue eyes were sharp, like her pointed nose. She was plain, but she was fit and carried herself with a great deal of self-confidence.

Maybe she has a little too much self-confidence. I thought.

"Pile in, pile in," Big Earl urged as he swung open the back door of the cab for us. Agent Bridge, Agent Stanton, and I climbed in the backseat of the cab, while Big Earl sat up front. Putting him up front was definitely the right decision based on his girth alone.

Our cab driver, Daniel, greeted us warmly, making us feel immediately welcomed. You could tell by Daniel's expression that he was excited to tell us about the history of his country, have a meal, and a paid fare for an entire day. The glint of joy and passion showed clearly in his brown eyes that peered at us through his lightly tinted glasses.

"Good morning, everyone," Daniel began, "Today we are going to travel about 85 miles up to the Sea of Galilee. We will stop in the town of Tiberias for lunch, and soak our feet in the River Jordan. Please, please ask me any questions as we travel today. I am most happy to be your guide, and I want you to enjoy your stay here in our wonderful country."

"Good morning," Big Earl replied. "We are looking forward to seeing some of your country as well."

As we drove north on Highway 2 Daniel explained that Israel had six districts and today we would be traveling from District four where Tel Aviv, then onto Districts three and two.

"We are very proud of our freeways here. The even numbered run north and south and the uneven run east and west. All of our signs, as you can see are in Hebrew, Arabic, and English."

"I didn't expect to see such modern highway," Jill commented as she looked out the window as the Mediterranean Sea whisked by as we traveled along the modern 8 lane highway.

"There's traffic here, just like we have in Los Angeles," Big Earl said.

"Yes, we have traffic, but it will grow less as we travel north away from Tel Aviv," Daniel replied.

We traveled from Tel Aviv to Haifa, and then onto Nazareth, and finally the town of Tiberius.

"We shall stop here for pictures," Daniel said as he pulled the taxi over at a turnout on Highway 77.

As we climbed out of the taxi we could see the vast Jordan Valley and the Sea of Galilee shimmering below us.

"Yes, the Sea of Galilee is below sea level," Daniel said as if on cue with reading our minds. "She is 686 feet below sea level. She is the lowest freshwater lake on earth."

"Wow, incredible. I've been to Death Valley in California, at the Badwater Basis and its only 282 feet below sea level there. I had no idea," I said as I shook my head in amazement.

Wait until I tell Sylvia about this. I thought. *She is going to be so jealous.*

Daniel volunteered to take our picture. He lined the four of us side-by-side with the Sea of Galilee sign behind us as proof that we were really there. Personally, I'm not a big fan of having my picture taken, but today I knew I was going to have as many pictures taken as I could in this land full of inspirations and holiness.

"Click away," I said to Daniel.

When we arrived at the shore, Daniel pointed out to us that much of the ministry of Jesus happened in and around this sea.

"Long, long ago there were settlements here and trade. It was a very popular place as it still is today," Daniel explained.

"Here it is said that Jesus walked on water, calming the stormy water, and feeding thousands of his followers with fish. Those are just a few of the stories about Jesus that occurred here," Daniel said with pride and enthusiasm.

"This is incredible," I said excitedly.

"Yes, it is a very remarkable place. And it is also the source of most of our drinking water for all of Israel.

"Wasn't part of the six-day war about water or rather the diversion of water?" Agent Stanton asked.

"Yes, water is and has been one of our significant conflicts with Lebanon, Syria, Jordan, Israel, and Palestine. We all need water, yet we cannot figure out how to compromise with one another," Daniel said.

Climbing back into the taxi, Daniel suggested that we drive down to the sea and then to the Jordan River where it believed that Jesus was baptized by John the Baptist.

"Incredible, incredible, incredible," I exclaimed as I put my feet into the River Jordan. "I cannot believe I am really here. I'm touching the same river bed that Jesus did."

Daniel smiled at my enthusiasm and went onto say, "Yes, and this is where Jesus was baptized."

"Wow, this is incredible." I was beginning to sound like a broken record but it was amazing to be where Jesus lived.

"This river runs north and south through the Sea of Galilee," Daniel said as we continued our tour. "Sadly, there is a great deal of ecological damage in the river due to the lack of cooperation between Israel, Jordan, and Syria."

"Is it kind of like the Jewish State of Israel versus the Arab States?" Jill asked.

"Yes, in many ways that is the root of many of our problems here. The diversion of water from the Jordan River has caused many problems for us and our surrounding countries, but we need the water for farming and agriculture."

"So somehow everyone needs to figure out how to get along?" I asked.

"Ah, yes, getting along. If only we could," said Daniel as we began walking back towards his taxi. "It's time for lunch my friends and a few more places to visit."

Once in Nazareth, Daniel guided us to a local restaurant where he wanted us to dine on a typical local meal of Tilapia Zilli, French fries, and a cabbage salad. We all readily agreed since it was early afternoon by now and we were famished.

During lunch we talked about visiting Capermaum and Tabgha.

"Capermaum is where Jesus, according to the Bible, healed a paralytic and where he also healed Peter's mother-in-law." Daniel stated as he sipped the water that the server had just poured into his glass.

"Isn't Tabgha where the Sermon on the Mount took place?" I asked.

"Yes, we'll drive by there and I'll point out the hill for you, but we'll not be able to drive up there today, for we are beginning to run out of time."

When lunch arrived, each plate contained a whole fish, eye ball intact and the skin fried to a crisp, scales and all.

"I'm not sure about this," I remarked to no one in particular.

"It is very good," Daniel said. "Please try it, let me show you how to eat this fish, bones, eyes and all."

Following Daniels advice, I peeled the skin back and carefully pulled the white Tilapia meat from the small, delicate bones of the fully cooked fish. The meat was tasty, it was not an oily fish like salmon, but dry and light, it was delicious.

"I have to admit, looking at a dead fish on my plate made me lose my appetite, but I'm glad I tried it."

"Good for you, Maggie, you've got to keep trying new things," Agent Stanton said. "Do you know, when I'm home I do most of the cooking for Roberta and the kids?"

"No, I didn't know that. How cool is that. Dave doesn't cook at all, I don't even think he can boil water," I said with a laugh. "I'm not sure what he does while I'm gone, take-out I bet."

Once we were back in the car, with a full stomach and the heat of the day warming up the taxi, this girl was ready for a nap.

Don't do it, Maggie, places still to go and people to see, I whispered inside my head.

As we headed back towards Tel Aviv, my mind ticked off everything we had seen and experienced that day.

"I think this is the most amazing place I have ever been," I said. "I am so glad we did this, you guys."

The hour and a half ride back to the hotel was a combination of banter about history, religion, water rights, and food. Daniel listened and watched as we interacted sometimes in loud voices and sometimes tame and respectful.

"We have arrived." Daniel said as we pulled into the enormous circular driveway in front of the hotel.

"Thank you," Agent Stanton said to Daniel as we all climbed out of the taxi.

"Yes, thank you so very much. This was the best tour I have ever been on," I said. "Thank you for spending so much time with us."

"It was my pleasure. I hope to see you all again someday. Enjoy the rest of your visit in our wonderful country." He said as he stepped away from the taxi and shook our hands.

"Here's a little extra for you," Agent Stanton said as he shook Daniel's hand and then everyone parted ways.

"Thank you and good-bye."

The four of us walked into the hotel lobby at 7 P.M.

Our departure time is 3 P.M. today so I have time for a run without a doubt," I said as I slipped on my running shoes. *I always work better after a long run.*

The city was bustling with activity by the time I stepped onto the warm cement sidewalk. I could run by the water here, there was a pedestrian path made for people to stroll, walk, or run along while looking out to the beautiful Mediterranean Sea.

As I ran, I reflected back on the magical day yesterday was. The imaged of the Sea of Galilee, the Jordan River, and the town of Nazareth danced through my head.

You're blessed beyond words, Maggie, I said out loud. *You are one lucky duck indeed.*

Later that afternoon, at the airport, our team stood for the second time in the long snaking lines that took us to the first document review station. Once our documents were checked and were in order, we proceeded to the second security checkpoint where we reached the stern faced agents. We were not only profiled visually, but verbally. The series of questions that we were asked were very detailed and specific.

After we cleared two security checkpoints, we finally reached the third checkpoint which was the x-ray screening machines.

"One more line, Maggie, and we'll be good as gold," Big Earl said.

"Yes, one more to go, and am I ready to go home," I replied.

Once we cleared the screeching magnetometers we met as a group and were escorted to a private lounge area where our firearms were returned to us in trade for the yellow slip each of us had been advised to hang onto when we surrendered our firearms upon entry into Israel.

"Did you know that this airport hasn't had any security threat penetrations since Israel implemented such a sophisticated security screening process?" Agent Stanton asked.

"I remember reading about their security systems in one of our recurrent training classes."

"These guys, or I should say gals since most of the security cadre here at the airport are ladies, have a specific set of questions they always ask, and they look for nerves or inconsistent statements." Stanton said.

"And without any doubt ethnicity does play a role here." I said.

Then Big Earl said, "You should think of this airport and its security systems as if each passenger had to pass through a concentric circle of security measures that get tighter and tighter as you get closer to the aircraft that you want to board. The fences, cameras, vehicle inspections, sensors, x-ray procedures, are all part of the security package at this airport. It's top notch."

And with that said we pre-boarded our aircraft for our returning flight to Paris and then home the following day.

"Good afternoon," Agent Lopez said while he was doing a head count to make sure we were all accounted for and ready to board.

"Just another day, Maggie, just another day," I whispered as I began conducting my portion of the aircraft search.

The entire team searched every portion of the aircraft before any of the passengers boarded. We search first class, business, and economy looking in the seat back pouches, tapping under each passenger seat, and peering into each over head bin. The lavatories were search with keen eyes and able hands to make sure no one had placed anything on that aircraft that wasn't supposed to be there.

Once the inspection was complete, Agent Lopez discussed with us where the least bomb location (LRBL) was for the type of aircraft we were flying on.

I remembered learning in our basic training that live-fire testing on pressurized single-aisle and wide body aircraft cabins had been conducted by the government to study locations or designs that will yield the least damage if a bomb found onboard an aircraft detonates.

During our training we had placed mock bomb and packed them with various materials to simulate what we would need to do if we ever found a bomb onboard an aircraft we were flying on.

Today, our aircraft search determined that there were no explosive devices onboard, but having a LRBL was a sound tactical approach to use in case one was discovered in-flight.

The Federal Aviation Administration (FAA) began implementing voluntary participation in the early 1970's, and our team was familiar with the locations on each aircraft that we flew, but it was standard protocol to review those locations on every flight.

Agent Lopez said, "I want each of you to go and physically look where the LRBL location is on this aircraft and then report back to me. I want confirmation that each of you knows where to go and what to do if we find a bomb onboard this bird."

Once the LRBL procedures were complete, we all took our seats and waited silently for passenger boarding to begin.

Check, check, it's time to go, Maggie. Home, sweet home - here I come!

CHAPTER 14

Home, Sweet Home

Landing at JFK felt like landing in heaven. The masses of population, noise, and pollution all greeted me with a "Welcome Home" hoorah. All of us were ready to get off airplanes for awhile and take a break. But only one team member was afforded that luxury, for the rest of us had to fly another segment to get to our final destinations.

After clearing customs and immigrations, we said our farewells and individually found a quiet location to secure our firearms and ammunition in our hard-sided luggage. Once stateside, we reverted back to regular civil servants and our firearms were no long authorized to be at our sides. I thought this was a ludicrous rule, but it was a rule that couldn't be compromised.

I found a bank of pay phones and decided to call Dave and let him know that I was back on U.S. soil. I had been gone for two and a half weeks so I was anxious to hear his deep, sweet voice again.

As I picked up the receiver, I dropped some coins in the phone, and dialed home. After four rings I hung the phone up.

Well, I'll have to wait a few more hours to hear his voice. I said with a sigh.

As I walked towards to the departure gate, I suddenly felt sick to my stomach.

I raced to the nearest ladies room and barely made it into a stall before I let go of my lunch.

Okay girl, what's gotten into you, I said as I looked at my pale face in the bathroom mirror. *Hope I can make it home.*

As I boarded the American Airlines flight, my legs felt wobbly, that would carry me home I felt out of sync, exhausted, and chilled. I was ready to get to home and rest.

When I stepped off my flight, I easily found my luggage waiting for me, but what I didn't find was a ride home.

I wonder where my hubby is.

As if on cue, he came rushing through the doors leading into the upper level baggage claim. "Hi Sweetie! Running late, but I'm here now."

"It's so good to be home," as we kissed and hugged.

"I have tomorrow off, but I have to go into the office on Thursday to get my travel voucher in, and see how much paperwork has piled up."

"I'm flying to Nashville tomorrow and then on down to the islands again," Dave said with a sad note in his voice.

"Well at least we have tonight, so we'll just have to make the best of it," I said.

"Yes, we will have to do that, Missy." He said as we left the airport strolling hand and hand.

The first thing I did when I woke up Wednesday morning was to head straight into the bathroom to get sick.

Here we go again Maggie.

"Are you okay Babe?" Dave inquired from behind the closed door.

"I think so, but something has got me. I threw-up yesterday afternoon too."

"Get to the doctor if you don't feel better later," Dave said.

"I will," I said as I opened the door and found my way back into bed. "I think I'll sleep a little longer this morning."

"Good idea, as for me, it's time to get ready for work," and with a peck on the top of my head, my husband took over the bathroom rights.

As I looked at my handsome husband, I knew how lucky I was to be married to such a terrific man. We had a very typical aviation life style, someone was either getting on or off an airplane, yet it was one of the common bonds that kept us together.

I closed my eyes and drifted off to sleep once again.

As I suspected, on Thursday, when I got to the office, my in-box was full.

"What a mess," I said, "but at least I'm home for awhile now."

"Hey, hey, welcome home," Randy said when he walked into the office later that morning. "How was your trip?"

"Long, but we saw some incredible sights, and racked up some pretty good overtime," I said as I looked up from my computer.

"How's it been around here?"

"Pretty dang quiet, except for all of the checkpoint failure cases that came in during the last week, especially out at Love Field," he said.

"Umm..."

"We're going to get asked to go out there the first of next week when President Bush comes into town." Randy continued.

"That's okay, I won't mind going out. Southwest Airlines and the airport staff are great to work with and are really cooperative. Plus, it's an easy ride home for me to get back up to Coppell." I said. "Just let me know what day and time, and I'll be glad to head out there."

"Thanks," Randy said with a big grin on his face, "it's my fifteenth wedding anniversary and I was planning on taking some leave before all of this came up, so now maybe I can after all."

"Glad to do it, Randy. You've sure helped me learn the ropes since I've been here. Besides, do you think anyone will notice that it's Maggie Stewart versus Randy Myers?"

"Ha, Ha, nope, not a chance," Randy said with a smile. "Thanks again."

Dallas Love Field is so much smaller than Dallas/Fort Worth International Airport. There is one major air carrier that has passenger service, Southwest Airlines. And there are several cargo airlines. The management team for both the airport and the airline are great people, always willing to accept the multiple security changes that have been required of them through the years, in particular the most recent with access control.

When the FAA implemented new access control procedures it impacted airports and airlines because card readers had to be installed on gates and doors that led from where passengers could go to where only airline employees were allowed. Now for the most part, employees had to wear identification badges and have access control proximity cards too.

When I arrived at the airport at 8 A.M., I was in luck, the space was open.

A perk for law enforcement is the airport operations department gave us a parking spot in front of the terminal, so we don't have to go hunting for parking unless another federal G-car got the parking spot first.

High five, I said as I tapped my hand on the steering wheel, *I'm in luck today*.

I grabbed my note pad, made sure I had my credential in my business suit pocket; I locked the G-car door and headed for the main terminal to spend some time monitoring the checkpoint. It was a cool and crisp morning; fall was beginning to descend on Texas like and it felt nippy but marvelous.

"Burr," I should have brought a coat."

When I arrived at the checkpoint it was empty. The morning bank of flights had already departed and the next flights were a few hours away.

"Since there aren't any passengers I'll head over to the airport manager's office. I'll be back later," I told the screening manager Jase.

"Okay, we'll see you later. We'll be looking for you now." He said with a smile.

"Yes, you will," I laughed back. "But as you can see I came empty handed today. No checkpoint testing for you guys. I just wanted to see how everything was going since I heard you had a pretty rough week last week with missing a few test."

"We did," Jase said, "but we've retained the screeners that failed and hopefully we'll do much, much better next time."

"Okay Jase, let's hope so. I'll see you later then."

When I got to Jim Stillwell's office, the airport manager, it was jammed with secret service agents.

President Bush was coming in today on Air Force One, I thought.

With my FAA Special Agent Credentials in hand, I indentified my-self and walked through the front office door.

"Hi Katie, it's looking pretty busy around here today," I said to the Airport Managers secretary.

"Sure is, Maggie," Katie said, "President Bush will be here in about twenty minutes and this place is a madhouse."

"I forgot the exact time, but my subconscious must have kicked in, so I'm glad I made it in time. Any issues so far?"

"Not that I know of, the receiving line will be heading ramp-side anytime now. Jim was gracious enough to let me stand in for him so I get to meet the President," Katie said. "And I'm pretty darn excited."

"Good for you. You've got a good boss," I said as I looked around the room to see who else would be joining the receiving line. I rec-ognized a few people, but for the most part this event looked pretty low key.

Katie and I chatted for a few more minutes before one of the se-cret service agents said, "Okay, let's get this party started. Everyone who is in the receiving line, follow me."

"Okay, here I go," Katie said as she got up from her desk. "Hey, come with me, I don't think anyone will mind."

"Really?" I said.

"Yep, come on, you've got your Airport Identification and creden-tial, who's going to say anything?"

"I'm game; I've never met the president before".

As I stepped through the open door and onto the ramp, the blustering fall wind wrapped around my body and I felt like a popsicle. I began to feel the wind biting at my face, hands, seeping through my thin jacket, and black slacks.

"Its okay, Maggie; I'm going to meet the President of the United States! I won't be cold for long."

As Katie and I stood by one another, I again looked around to see who else was out on the ramp. Secret service, airport police, various airport personnel, and contract service personnel dotted the cement, oil stained ramp. A red carpet covered those ugly blemishes – as if to say, no President will have to tread on my soiled ground. Fire trucks, police cars, unmarked cars, and tugs dotted the ramp as well. Everyone and everything waited in silence.

When the B747 came around the corner, her engines whining, you could feel the electricity and excitement in the air. The ramp agent, wands in hand, began directing this beautiful aircraft towards the awaiting dignitaries; the Major of Dallas, city council members, prominent business leaders, and a few airport staff. The tail of the 747 reached stoically into the crisp air, the equivalent of a six-story building. She was magnificent! As her eighteen tires moved towards us, four under each wing, eight on the under carriage, and two at the nose gear, I felt her creating a vibration all the way down into the soles of my shoes as she moved across the tarmac. I heard nothing but jet engines, smelled the fumes of aviation gasoline, and immediately remembered why I loved this job so much.

"Magical, it's magical without any doubt."

As the ramp agent raised his arms and crossed the bright orange wands, forming an 'x', the aircraft came to a complete stop and the flurry of ramp agents plugging in APU units, driving tugs with baggage carts, and towing stairs to the forward left side of the aircraft began.

This normal flurry of activity took place under the ever watchful eyes of every law enforcement agent there. This was a time the aircraft and the President were vulnerable, even though all of the personnel, trucks and content were searched well in advance of this aircraft's arrival.

Well, they are supposed to be. Let's hope everything was done right, I thought.

The presidential staffer assigned to ensure the receiving line was in order began making sure everyone was in position to receive the President, First Lady, and the additional staff. Again, I could feel the excitement mounting in the air as everyone got ready for this historic moment.

Once again, I briefly scanned the ramp to see if anything looked unusual. I saw the airport manager, Jim Stillwell looking directly at me. He was standing about 25 yards away, leaning on a tug, surrounded by a couple of airport operations employees.

He mouthed, "What are you doing there?"

I shrugged my shoulders, smiled, and mouthed back, "Beats me."

Jim just shook his head in disbelief that I was standing in the receiving line to meet the President of the United States and I was not on any official list.

As the main door of Air Force One swung open several ground crew personnel began rolling the jet way stairs to the aircraft with swift precision and care.

"Don't hurt that aircraft, Mack," I heard one of the ramp rats say.

"I won't Gus, for christsakes, you know I've been doing this for fifteen years. It's just another day at work as far as I'm concerned."

"Well there'll be hell to pay if we screw this up," Gus hollered as he continued to watch Mack with an eagle eye.

Once the stairs were in place, I could see the President poised in the doorway waiting to be given the cue to descend.

I was awe struck. I've never been this close to any President. "Wait until I tell Dave about this," I said to no one in particular.

When the President Bush and the First Lady were off the aircraft, the multiple greetings and handshakes were completed with precision and hast. There was minimal time allotted for meeting and greeting, but a few seconds were better than none.

President Bush shook my hand and moved quickly to the next guest. His handshake was strong and warm.

First Lady Bush stopped next and shook my hand. She looked me up and down, and then asked: "Young lady, where is your coat? It's freezing out here."

"I left it at home," I uttered.

"Remember it next time," she said as she smiled, patted my hand, and moved on to shake someone else's waiting hand.

"Wow, wow, the First Lady of the United States shook my hand and she spoke to me. What a Mom she is, worrying about whether I had a jacket on or not," I thought.

"How the heck did you get in the receiving line?" Jim Stillwell asked once the presidential limo and the secret service detail departed through the non-terminal side of the airport.

"I went up to see you and I saw Katie instead. One thing led to another, and well, no one told me I couldn't, so I did."

"Well, well this is one for the history books; just don't site us for a security breach, okay?"

"I won't." I said.

During the drive back to the office, the local news channel was advising drivers of the various street closures due to the recent arrival of President George W. Bush and First Lady Barbara Bush.

I was still in awe that I had shaken the hand of the 41st President of the United States and that Mrs. Bush cared enough to ask a stranger where her coat was.

Fortunately, when I got back to the office I only had thirty minutes left on the clock. I was still so excited; I knew my concentration to do any paperwork was pretty much shot for the day.

Sitting at my desk, looking out the window, I saw cows off in the distance and the flicker of lightening. It was time to get those cows in for the evening, I thought. And, it was time to get myself in for the evening as well. The combination of feeling excited and exhausted at the same time was new to me, but I definitely knew I was both.

On the way home I stopped at Kroger's to pick up some groceries for the next couple of days, comfort food that I liked since Dave was flying and he wouldn't be home until next week, a new Runner's Magazine.

I hadn't been feeling well for the past few weeks, no chills, no fever, but I felt like I had the flu. And then I missed my period. Passing the first aid, dental care, and shampoos, I stopped by the personal hygiene section and picked up a pregnancy kit.

Holding the kit in my hand, I thought. *I suspect this will tell you what's going on Maggie.*

Part III

CHAPTER 15

A Few Years Later

A few years ago as I held the pregnancy kit in my hand and thought: *This might tell you what's going on Maggie,* proved to tell me exactly what was happening.

Monica Irene was born the following February at 8 pounds and 12 ounces. It was a long labor, twenty-two hours, but worth every push. Then twenty-two months later to the day, on a mild December afternoon, Michael David was born at 8 pounds 10 ounces. After having a girl and a boy it was time to stop – no more children for us.

Aunt Frances and Uncle Roger, as we fondly called them now loved our kids as much as we did. They didn't have any kids and they weren't married, but if there were any two people that were meant for one another it was Frances and Roger.

"Scooter, come here buddy," Aunt Frances would say to Michael. Miss Monica was a tall and thin for her age so we called her Bean.

At 6 A.M. I dropped Monica and Michael off at the Children's World Day Care that was almost directly outside of the townhomes on Samuel Blvd where we lived.

Holding Monica's hand and carrying Mike, I said, "I love you guys, and I'll see you later. Have fun and be good today," I said while hugging, kissing, and them handing them off to the caregiver that was waiting in the colorful lobby.

Pulling out of the parking lot, I turned on the radio to hear the news, and mentally began getting organized for the day. There was a light mist in the air, so I turned on my headlights and windshield wipers.

I had been with security almost 6 years, and today I would know if I was selected for the supervisory position I had bid on and interviewed for. If I was selected I would be promoted from a GS-12 to a GS-13, which meant a significant pay raise and a lot more responsibility.

The Government Scale (GS) pay system contains fifteen GS levels that you promote to, and ten steps with-in each GS level. If you received an acceptable annual performance review, you would automatically be promoted to the next with-in step increase for the first four years within that band. If you got a promotion you would skip some pay levels all together. The system sounded complicated, but it really wasn't. However, one of the significant factors in the federal service retirement system was that your pension was based on your annual salary. So it was important to progress through the federal pay system to the highest level you could.

I was more than ready for the responsibility, less travel, and of course a pay raise is always a good thing.

I'm ready.

Dave had hired on with the FAA last year as a Flight Standards Inspector as a GS-12, so we were both making good money. Yet for some reason we were fighting more and more. And his job took him overseas for long stretches at a time which didn't help our marriage. Every time he returned home, he seemed more and more disengaged with the family.

I can't get a handle on why we are fighting so much. I pondered with a mix of anger and sadness. *We've both worked so hard, yet we don't appreciate what we have…at least it seems that way. Okay, worry about Dave on the way home, right now, you've got stuff to worry about at work.*

The freezing drizzle had just started as I pulled into the office parking lot on Fuller-Wiser Road. I got out of my car, grabbed my briefcase, jacket, and carefully walked to the covered stairs that led to the second-story.

Tucked safely in the warm, cozy building I shook myself off and proceeded to my office.

"Hi, ya," Randy said.

I sat down at my desk and turned on my computer. "Morning, you're in early today. What's up?"

"Got some inspections on Oklahoma City later this afternoon and I'm going to be there all week. So figured I'd get a jump on the day, and get the last minute paperwork done before I head out."

"Well, be careful, snow is on its way I suspect from how it looks and feels outside this morning." I said.

"I know," Randy said, "I-35 is already jammed packed, and it's only 730 A.M."

"And you Texans tell us L.A. traffic is bad," I said with a sly grin.

At 8:00 A.M., the office intercom system beeped indicating that an announcement was soon to commence. Sure enough, the office secretary's voice blasted over the intercom system: "Good morning everyone, please plan on attending a brief all-hands meeting in the conference room in thirty-minutes. Thank you."

"Well so much for leaving at 8:30," Randy said.

"Sounds like it will be a short one, so I bet you can leave at 8:45!"

At 8:30 A.M. everyone gathered in the conference room, warm mugs of coffee in hand, and a box of donuts on the table. I smiled as I looked around the room.

Some things never change, no matter where you are, I thought. *Coffee and donuts - got to love it!*

Office Manager, David Flowers, and Supervisor, Nelda Michaels, both had donuts in their hands as they greeted us.

"No need to even a grab chair guys, this won't take long," David advised the agents.

I looked over at Randy and winked, a wink that said, *See I told you you'd be out of here lickety split.*

"As you know, Nelda was selected as the Deputy Division Manager for the Southwest Region and we haven't seen too much of her since her promotion." Glancing at Nelda, David continued, "And she has been gracious enough to try and keep both jobs; the one here, and her new position at the regional office-until the position here was filled. Well today, I'd like to announce who the new supervisor for the DFW CASFO is going to be."

I held my breath in anticipation; seven people had bid on the position, so it was anyone's guess on who was going to be selected. I hoped it was me, but I just didn't know.

"So without further ado, I am pleased to announce that one of our own has been selected", he paused, and then said "Maggie Stewart will become your supervisor effective the next pay period."

Clapping and words of congratulations filled the room.

"Thanks everyone, thanks!" I said. I was so happy. I was really looking forward to the opportunity to move into management.

"Okay, that's it from me. Get back to work. Maggie come see me in my office, please." David said, waving his hand in the air, in an attempt to scoot everyone from the conference room.

"Way to go, Maggie," Randy said giving me a high-five on his way out the door. "I've been with the feds 7 years now and I'm planning on staying an agent forever. Management just isn't my cup of tea. So I guess you're about to be my new boss. I'm off to do some inspections...see you later."

"Thanks, Randy...later."

Several hours later, when I returned to my office, there was a sticky note on my chair: Agent Stanton had called from Los Angeles.

As I picked up the phone to call him, I was excited to tell him the news of my pending promotion. Last year, he had accepted a supervisory position in L.A. and had occasionally called or emailed me to tell me how it was going. He seemed happy with his new position and said he didn't miss the FAM program. Less travel, more time at home, was better for him and his family.

The policy in the FAA was that once you became a supervisor or manager you would no longer participate in the air marshal program. Mainly because the FAM program required a lot of travel, recurrent training twice a year in Arizona, and then multiple missions that took you away from the office for two to three weeks at a time. Being gone so much was a significant burden on the office. So, as a rule-of-thumb, once you moved into management, you moved out of the FAM program.

I was looking forward to my new responsibilities, and yes, less travel. More time with the family would be wonderful too.

"Hey there," Stanton said. "I just heard congratulations."

"How the heck did you hear so soon? I was going to call and surprise you."

"Oh you know me, I have spies everywhere."

"Well darn, no surprise for you, but thanks. I'm stoked." I said.

"I bet you are. You'll have tons of paperwork now, Maggie."

"I know, but that's okay, I'm ready."

"Okay, I'm happy for you. Got to go, I've got an airport meeting in about fifteen minutes. Say Hi to Dave and the kids for me."

"Likewise to Roberta and the kids, Lee," I said and then hung up the phone with a grin on my face.

As I looked out the window, the freezing drizzle had turned to snow. The parking lot and the cars were slowing blending into a beautiful sea of white. I hoped Randy was safely out of town and driving on the open stretches of I-35 North. I, on the other hand, knew my commute later today was going to be a mess!

Texans aren't use to driving in snow. I think they are crazy drivers under normal conditions, so I wasn't looking forward to my drive home later.

Nope, it's going to be a mess today, so be prepared! I thought.

I wanted to call Dave and tell him the good news, but I didn't have the telephone number of the hotel where he was staying in Paris.

Dave had left Monday for a four week trip in France to work on the final FAA Proving Runs Certifications for the Airbus. He was traveling with a team of three other inspectors: two men and one woman, all from Washington.

I knew they had a hectic schedule to meet. Dave had told me a few weeks before he left that they were woefully behind, not their fault, because someone in Washington, D.C., had dropped the ball. Unfortunately, the airlines needed the certification timeline to stay intact to meet customer demands. That pretty much left Dave and his fellow team members jumping through hoops in France.

Or at least, I thought that's what they were doing.

CHAPTER **16**

Left Behind In Paris

I never really appreciated Paris during my travels there because the citizens were aloof and rude-more rude than aloof-and they didn't seem to like Americans at all. I'm a people person so I was more sensitive to their dislike for us than most of my team. Yet, I did appreciate their architecture. It was superb. Their museums' were a marvel to visit, their churches to pray in, and older their buildings were lovely in every way. And of course their wines, well what can I say. Their wines were splendid in every way.

"Let's get another bottle," Dave said half way through dinner. He was dining at a small restaurant in Paris with his colleagues.

"That's a splendid idea. That red was marvelous," Becky said while everyone at the table nodded their heads in agreement.

The server opened and poured more wine as meals, conversation, and laughter carried them into the late hours. Late enough that the manager of the restaurant told them that it was time for them to pay their bill, for it was past closing time.

"What a great meal, I needed this, especially after the incredibly frustrating day we've had," Becky said while walking back to their hotel. "I'm not sure we're going to make our deadline this week," she continued on.

"Yes, we're definitely behind schedule," Tyrone said affirming Becky's earlier concerns.

"Well, what do we do about it?" asked Dave.

"First, we talk to Airbus in the morning to see what we can do to get the changes we need completed. If that happens then we'll be able to get the Flight Certification Process underway. But we need the airworthiness items repaired and checked-off before we can go any further," advised Becky.

Everyone agreed. Becky knew this team was working well together and they were a good match. Dave was the field expert, a pilot, and the newest member to join the FAA. Becky was an operations manager in Washington, D.C., and Nevil was on her team there. Tyrone was an airworthiness expert, also from D.C., but was here specifically to address the very few remaining mechanical issues that held the Airbus up from getting FAA Approval to starting flying under any U.S. Flagship Certificate.

The team, in actuality, had been pressured into traveling to France because the U.S. Airlines that had advance purchases for the Airbus were beginning to complain, actually, scream that the aircraft was not getting certified by the FAA quickly enough.

The FAA was caught between a rock and a hard spot in that, yes, they were responsible for getting the aircraft U.S. certified, but it was the responsibility of France and the Air Bus Manufactures to fix the identified repairs.

"Basically, it's a mess," Becky said, "but somehow we've got to fix it, and fix it fast, or we'll all be looking for new jobs."

"So we're half way through this trip, and we've only got about twenty-five percent done so far," Tyrone said.

"That's an accurate assessment. I always knew you were intelligent," Becky said with a hint of irony in her voice.

As the team approached the hotel, Dave said, "Well, we'll see what tomorrow brings."

In the lobby, everyone said good night before heading to their rooms with the agreement to be in the lobby at 8 A.M. It was well past midnight so sleep was going to be precious tonight.

In his room, Dave saw the call button light blinking. After dialing voicemail he heard Maggie's voice saying,

"Hi Dear, checking in to see how you're doing. All is well here. The kids are fine. I have some good news to tell you, so call me when you get in."

Looking at his watch, Dave made a mental note of the time and knew that Maggie was already at work.

"I'll call her tonight," he said as he climbed into bed.

The following day, in fact the following week, proved to be more troublesome than the past two weeks. Schedules slipped, people's tempers rose, and overall not very much was accomplished.

"Well team, we're at week three. I suggest we extend our travel orders and stay for two more weeks. I think we're close, so if we pull out now, we may be starting all over again." Becky told the team at dinner.

"I've cleared the extension with everyone but your wives gentlemen. So I suggest you call home this evening and see if you can extend for two more weeks without getting divorced." She said.

"Its work," Dave said, "that's why it's a four letter word. My wife will understand since she's a 'fed' too."

"Hi Sweetie, how's it going there? How are the kiddos?" Dave said as soon as I answered the phone.

"Good, good, how are you stranger? It's been almost a week now since I've heard from you. Are you in France or Africa?" I said with a tiny hint of sarcasm.

"What do you mean? You know I'm in Paris Maggie." Dave said defensively.

"Yes, I do, but since you are so hard to get a hold of, I thought you might have been given another assignment. Perhaps you're in Africa where it's harder to phone home and see how your family's doing."

"Gosh, you of all people should know how it is when you travel. Time zones, work schedules, things just get messed up. I can't begin to tell you how busy I've been."

"I know, I know, so how's it going?" I said trying to cheer and be a more understanding wife.

"Bad. We've been asked to stay two more weeks." Dave said in a hurried voice. "D.C. has cleared it, but our team leader wants to make sure our families are copacetic with it too. I want to know that it's okay too. It's a long time to be away from home."

"I can't say I like it, but it's the way it is. I know when I get extended it's for a good reason so I know you need to stay too Dave."

"Thanks, Missy," a nickname he rarely used anymore, "I knew you'd understand. And think of the per diem we're making."

"I would, but somehow I suspect there won't be much left," I said to myself as I hung up the phone. I knew what a bottle of fine wine cost in France. And I knew my husband would only drink the very best when given the opportunity. Dave had many, many wonderful qualities, but saving money was not one of them.

I didn't get the chance to tell him about my promotion either.

Peeking in the kids' room I smiled as I saw their tiny chests rising and falling as they slept. *It's time for you to get some sleep to girl.* "And remember to get to Mass tomorrow." I said as I climbed into bed, alone once again, tired from another long day. Being a single mom was hard; especially when you weren't suppose to be one.

Four weeks turned into six weeks and then into eight weeks before Dave finally stepped onto Texas soil.

"Whoa, you look incredible," Dave said as he kissed and hugged me while his two children clung to his knees. Mike was just beginning to walk and Monica was already in the full-speed-ahead mode. She was getting into mischief with every step too.

"You look pretty darn good yourself Dear."

After dinner and tucking the kids in, I said, "alone at last.", as

I nuzzled close to Dave. Feeling the steady heart beat beneath his shirt I wanted to go upstairs and tear his clothes off. Two months was a long time to be alone. But instead, for the next couple of hours Dave talked about work, France, the team he was with, the Airbus. He didn't say one word about missing us.

"Come on, Honey, let's go upstairs. I've missed you. Plus I have to work tomorrow so I'll need to get some sleep tonight. You are the lucky one who gets the day off tomorrow."

"I'll be up in a minute. I'm going to check my email real quick." Dave said as he gave me a peck on the top of my head.

Really, I'm that far down on his list of priorities now. I said to my-self almost in tears. I mumbled "K, see you in a bit," as I climbed the stairs to our bedroom alone once again.

At 4:45 A.M., my Sandhill crane alarm reminded me once again that it was time to get up and get to the office. I looked at Dave, flat on his back, sound asleep to the world, and decided to hit the snooze alarm for another eight minutes of blissful sleep. Dave was home today, after two months of travel. Since he traveled through so many time zones to get home, he was allotted 8 hours of paid administrative time to readjust to Central Standard Time. And if he was smart he'd take tomorrow, Friday off, as an annual leave day, and make it a four day weekend.

Wishing I could do the same thing, but knowing I couldn't, I hit the snooze alarm again. I had a project due Friday for D.C., which was finished yet, and I wasn't able to extend the suspense date.

On the way to the office, I pounded the steering wheel and shout-ed, "What the hell happened in France?" Flipping on my turn signal, I turned right onto Bass Pro Road towards the freeway. *Bad, it has to be something bad. Soon I'm going to have to find out what happened... but I'm not sure I want to know.*

The work weeks came and went. Dave and I got partially back on track, he went into the regional office everyday in Ft. Worth and I continued to drive to the office in Euless. We dropped off and picked up kids, ran errands, saw Helen and Roger often, and got back to normal. Everything was back to normal except making love. Too busy, too something, everyday it was something. And that something had ever so slightly shifted our relationship.

"Okay, it's time to meet the beast," I said while standing in the kitchen before Dave got home. Monica and Mike were happily feasting on mac and cheese, cantaloupe, and vanilla wafers. "Yes, I know it's all the same color, but I just didn't care. They are happy, so I am happy."

"Well, let me know if you need anything. I'll bring wine over anytime day or night or a baseball bat, your choice," Helen, Aunt Frances as well call her now, said with a wicked smile and a fisted hand shaking in the air.

"Thanks, Sweetie. I'll let you know what's going on as soon as I know. But something has got to give. It's been months now and I just can't figure this out."

"You will, you're Special Agent Maggie Stewart, you can figure anything out." she said as she hugged me.

"Hey, where are your shoes?" I hollered.

"At home, bye Monica and bye to you, Scooter, love you."

"Crazy girl," I hollered as she walked out the door.

I knew I had to tell Dave about my upcoming FAM mission too. Earlier at the office my boss, David Flowers had told me that I was scheduled for an air marshal mission and I'd be gone almost three weeks.

"I know this is unusual since you've been in management for the last six months, but the agency has lost a lot of FAMS to management positions in the past year and the training academy at Marana won't have its next graduating class for another month. So they've asked for a couple of supervisors from each region, and you're currently the only FAM in management in the Southwest region. So, I can release you Maggie, and know that D.C. really needs the bodies."

"It's okay. Do you know where I'm going and for how long?" I asked.

"Ten day trip to South America but I don't know what countries."

"Well that's a new stamp for the passport. I've haven't been anywhere in South America yet."

After Dave and I finished eating, I began clearing the table, leaving the dishes soaking in the sink, which is something I never did. But tonight I needed to find out what was going on. I needed to find out why our relationship was rocky. I had to figure out what the heck was going on in our marriage. And I had to tell my aloof husband that I would be traveling again as a marshal.

With a dry tongue, sweaty palms, and a beating heart, I began with, "Honey, we need to talk."

"Uh oh," was the audible response from my husband.

"Let's go sit on the back patio." I walked back into the kitchen, opened the patio sliding glass door, and stepped onto our little patio.

Dave lit his pipe as we sat down. I sat at the small table, facing Dave and I said in almost a whisper, "I need to know what's going on Honey. Ever since you came back from France, you haven't been the same. Our love making has come to almost a complete halt, you barely take any interest in how I dress, what I talk about, how works going, and needless to say you've been very impatient with Monica and Michael. What's wrong?"

"Well, I guess it's time to talk about this," Dave said as he puffed on his pipe. "Maggie shortly before we left Paris, Becky offered me a job in D.C.," he continued. "Becky said I was the team's bright spot and the savior of the Airbus project; meaning that I was a problem solver, a go getter, and D.C. desperately needs me. She needs me on her team; she wants me to move to D.C."

"Is this work or love, Dave? Do you love her?" I asked.

"No, it's nothing like that. I just feel stale in my job here. I need more, I need challenges, more adventure, more travel. I miss the international arena. I want to take the job in D.C. Maggie."

"What about us, Dave? Isn't being married, having two incredible kids, a wife, and a GS-13 enough?" I asked completely shocked.

"What about my career? I can't quit, I can't transfer. I've already made one transfer for us Dave. What do you expect from me?"

Dave looked at me with his big eyes, and sadly said, "I'm so sorry. I never meant to hurt you Maggie."

"That's it? You're sorry?" Then and there I knew that our marriage was over. The kids and I were about to be left alone, alone to find our own way.

I stood, walked inside and headed upstairs to check on the kids, and then to my bedroom. I sat on the bed, placing the palms of my hands to my face and cried. I cried until there were no more tears to shed.

I picked up the phone and called my sister. Between huge sobs, I blurted out, "Dave's leaving me Sis. Can you believe it? He leaving me for another...job."

CHAPTER **17**

The Final Mission

As we gathered outside the American Airlines Terminal at DFW Airport, we looked like a flock of Ring-billed Gulls, standing on cement, but wishing our feet were standing in wet sand rather than the gum spotted, dull, scratched sidewalk.

But one team member wasn't there. Ironically, Agent Lopez was our team leader again, and I thought he was going to explode even before we got inside the terminal.

"Oh, good grief," he kept saying while looking at his watch. "We're going miss this flight, and D.C. is going to be pissed."

Agent Randy Myers almost flew out of the car when his wife pulled up to the curb. "I'm sorry, I'm sorry, I'm sorry," he said. "We were on our way here and little Randy suddenly threw-up in the car, of course all over me, so we had to go home so I could change; change or else you would have really hated me."

"I don't want to hear it, let's go." Agent Lopez roared.

As we approached the ticket counter I think the ticket agent could sense the frustration building in Agent Lopez. He didn't walk to the counter, he stomped up to it. He moved in full fury, even though no one else was responsible for his anger except himself.

I looked down at my wrist watch and I knew we still had plenty of time to make the flight, even pre-board before the passengers.

"We still have time." I said.

"Guess I really pissed Lopez off." Randy said as he slipped in beside me.

"Yep, and it looks like you did a very good job of it too."

"Okay, give me your documents and discreetly check your gear so we can get going ASAP," Lopez ordered.

While we handed Lopez our passports, I doubled checked my gear and started getting myself prepared for the long flight from Dallas to Caracas, Venezuela.

"Oh shit! Oh shit, I can't believe it," I heard Randy screech out in a frog's voice. "Oh shit."

"Now what," yelled Lopez as he turned around and looked at Randy.

"My gun, it's not here. It must have fallen out in the car when my kid got sick. Oh shit."

"I can't believe I'm flying with a bunch of morons. Are you F'ing kidding me Myers? I swear I'm going to kill you if this is true."

Randy hung his head while shaking from side to side.

I haven't seen too many grown men cry, but I thought I might be a witness to this unusual event any moment now.

"For God's sake, get a hold of your wife, and get this taken care of now. And I mean now." Lopez hollered.

As Lopez turned back to the agent, she processed the rest of the team and held Randy's papers aside just in case. In case he actually missed the flight and, if so, there would be hell to pay.

"I'll be right back. I'm going to the ladies room." I said before anyone could tell me no. I needed a break from the tension that was mounting. Randy was my office partner, and I hated to see him embarrassed like this, but I knew he was responsible for himself, and he'd have to figure it out.

Right now, I just needed more space and more air. I walked a few short yards to the ladies restroom.

Returning to the ticket counter, I heard Lopez instructing the team to follow the airline agent assigned to escort us to the aircraft behind the airline ticket counter.

"You're on your own, Myers," Lopez said. "If your wife gets here on time and you retrieve your gun, you'll have to go through screening and follow the normal law enforcement procedures for carrying a firearm onboard. If you make it in time, I'll deal with you later. If you miss the flight, I'll still deal with you later. But now I need to get what's left of this team onboard."

"You understand?"

"Yes sir."

"Let's go." then Lopez and the rest of the team disappeared behind the ticket counter and into the bowels of the airport, maneuvering through narrow hallways, beneath dusty, dirty conveyor belts carrying cargo and luggage, and noisy, screaming machinery that worked 24/7 to keep the airplanes that arrived and departed from this gate on time. I dusted off a cob-web that stuck to my sunglasses as I passed through this restricted area – restricted meaning you needed to either be escorted into this area by someone with an airport identification badge or have one of your own.

For all our sake, I hope Randy makes this flight. I said looking up towards the sky and whispering a silent prayer: *Help him Lord. Randy really needs some help right about now.*

The American Airlines agent introduced our team leader to the Captain said his good-byes to us. As I watched the agent trot away, I was convinced that he was very, very relieved to be rid of us.

Thinking to myself I thought: *Heck, I'd want to be rid of us too, after this debacle of a check-in process.*

After introductions were made, we quickly climbed the stairs leading to the jet way bridge and the forward cabin of the aircraft. Once the aircraft search was made, Agent Lopez gave us our seat assignments. I was back in the economy section for this flight. *Back of the pack is all right with me for a change.*

I walked all the way aft, put my backpack under the seat in front of me, and pushed it all the way forward and to the left. This way I'd have some room to stretch out my feet now and again. I stuffed one of the paperback books I had with me in the seat pocket in front of me. And, as the passengers began to board, I watched, waited, and observed as people stuffed their luggage into the closest overhead bin they could find that still had room.

My mind began shifting as I looked at people differently – good guy, bad guy – who to watch and who to assume might be all right. *Don't assume too much Maggie, because you just never know.* I silently reminded myself.

I also wondered where Randy was. Did he make the flight? Did he miss it? Was our team intact, or were we one member short? Would this create a vulnerability that would need attention?

Lopez will let us know when he can. I thought.

The flight attendants performed the security briefings in English and Portuguese, so the briefings lasted longer that those given on domestic flights, and I could tell that we were also taxiing at a slower rate of speed so the crew would have plenty of time to finish up. Once the flight attendants were seated I knew that we were just about ready to take off.

Thirty-five minutes into the flight, I saw Agent Lopez make his way to the rear lavatory and covertly signal that Myers had made the flight. It was good to have the full cadre onboard.

Good, thank you Lord. I whispered.

When we landed in Caracas, we deplaned with the rest of the passengers and proceeded towards customs and immigrations.

After clearing customs, we stood outside the terminal to wait for the hotel shuttle. Our ground time of barely 12 hours would be repeated daily, with the same procedures for the next ten days. The only saving grace was that we'd have five nights here in Caracas and five nights in Dallas. Five nights in Dallas meant I'd be home for half of this mission, a first for me.

"We're in luck on this trip, Randy," I said as we boarded the hotel shuttle. "At least, we'll be home for half the trip nights, less per diem than the rest of the team, but I'll take time with my kids any day over money."

"Yep, I'm happy for that too. Glad I live in Bedford." Randy remarked.

"I'm at the opposite end of the airport, but living in Coppell works for me." I said with a great big grin.

The ride to the hotel took twenty minutes, and I looked out the window as we drove along the crowded streets of Caracas. I thought about all the changes ahead for me: a dissolved marriage, raising two kids on my own, and my family was in California. But then I realized that I had friends here, a new position as a manager, and a safe, economical place to live.

And I thought, *what the hell was Dave thinking? What, if anything could I have done differently to make his stay?* I wanted to cry, but I knew I couldn't. *"Save those tears for another time Maggie."*

Dave, my husband, soon to be ex-husband, did accept a staff job in Washington, D.C. and he was moving in two weeks. I couldn't believe it, but it was true. A GS-14 job was more important than his wife and two kids.

I'm partly to blame too. I thought. *I transferred once for Dave, but I wasn't willing to ask again, especially since I had just been promoted to a supervisory position. Asking a second time would be career suicide. So I didn't ask, I just let him go.*

"It's what I need to do Maggie," he told me over the phone. He had already moved out. "But I'll stay and watch the kids while you're on your trip. I'll pick the kids up from school, feed them, you know, do the whole dad thing, and then drop them off the next morning at day care before I head to the office. You'll have to get them at night after your trips."

"Thanks, Dave, that's just swell," I said my voice dripping with sarcasm. "But actually Aunt Frances is going to pick them up from day care for me, because by the time I land, clear customs, and drive home, the center will be closed."

"Oh, okay," he said.

"You bastard." I said after we hung up.

The Venezuela Marriott Hotel Playa Grande was not right on the beach, but the view from my room of the ocean was stunning.

Since we didn't have any in-flight incidents our team briefing was quick, efficient. I knew I'd have at least thirty minutes to swim before I'd want dinner. I had a pounding headache so I hoped the warm water would ease my throbbing temples. I was tired, frustrated, and sad about my home life, but I knew I needed to stay focused and get through this mission.

Back in my room, while changing into my bathing suit, I said, "Oh, you are so beautiful, you Caribbean Sea, you". I opted to swim rather than go for a run because the front desk clerk recommended not leaving the hotel unless you were escorted. The clerk explaining that is a great hotel but it's not in a particularly good area of town.

I only swam for about twenty minutes due to the invasion of about 15 teenagers of various ages and ability to yell. They immediately jumped in the pool, splashing each other, screaming and laughing the whole time.

"Time to get out of here," I said as I quickly climbed out of the pool, grabbed my towel, slipped my shorts and flip flops on and headed for the elevator.

"I'd like to order a dinner salad, garlic and shrimp pasta, and two glasses of chardonnay please," I told room service.

They repeated my request, "Thank you," I said hanging up the phone.

Flipping on the TV, I switched from the hotel welcome channel to CNN. Far, far away as I watched the television, I immediately sit down on the bed feeling both shock and anger.

It was February 27, 1993, and the news reporter was talking about the unfolding events in New York City. An explosion had occurred a few hours ago at the World Trade Center. Images of rescue vehicles responding to the scene filled the TV screen. The bomb had instantly cut off the main electrical power, which in turn had knocked out the emergency lightening system, which made rescue efforts even harder. Smoke was rising through the building, filling the stairs, which made evacuating people by fire officials very, very difficult.

I watched in silence, only stepping away for just a few minutes to answer the door when room service arrived with my dinner.

"When are we ever going to find peace in this world?" I asked myself.

The following morning, a news paper that had been slipped under my door, showed horrific photos of the World Trade Center One bombing. Six people were killed, one of them being a woman who was seven months pregnant. The article mentioned that the immediate cause was a transformer explosion, but in case it was an act of terrorism, agents and bomb technicians from the AFT, FBI, and NYPD had quickly responded to the scene.

Onboard our flight, I said, "It's terrible about New York. Lopez is checking in constantly with D.C. to see if our orders are going to change, but no news yet. Flexibility is the name of the game in this job."

"That's for sure. We're half way through this mission," Randy said as we stood in the very back of the plane on our final leg of the day from Caracas to Dallas.

"Yes, we are, we'll see what happens."

"How's your back today?" Randy asked.

"Better today, and at least when we're all the way aft in coach we can stand-up like we are now, and not compromising our positions. The seats are terrible, even more than usual."

"I feel your pain, girl," Randy said.

When I got home, Aunt Frances greeted me with a glass of wine and a big hug, "Whoa, it looks like you need this glass of wine, Sweetie."

"I do indeed. Thanks for watching the kids for me and I'm sorry that I'm really late tonight," I said.

"No problem, better than watching Roger sleep!"

"Thanks for the wine. What a day, but only two more days and we're done with this trip," I sighed.

"Well, I love you, girl. Kids are fed, had their baths and I even read to them. They were happy campers when I tucked them in," Helen said updating me on my kids' activities for the day.

"You are a gem, love you." I said while closing the door after Aunt Frances as she headed across the parking lot to her place.

The late night news said that Mohammad Salameh had been arrested earlier in the day in New York and was being charged for the bombing of the World Trade Center.

After the bombing, investigators surveyed the damage and obviously went looking for clues as to what caused the explosion. While combing through the rubble in the underground parking area, a bomb technician located some internal components from the vehicle that was thought to have delivered the bomb to the building on that dreadful February day. The investigators found a vehicle identification number and a piece from an axle that led them to a Ryder truck rental operating in New Jersey.

Sadly the pieces are coming together, terrorism once again, Maggie. This is why you do what you do for a living girl.

I climbed the stairs, looked in on my kids, and sipped my wine while I walked to my bedroom, "I'm more than ready to call it a day. I'm exhausted," I said, "but two more days and this mission will be over."

The final two days of the mission were exhausting. The flights to and from Caracas were packed with families, tourists, business professionals, and air marshals. The World Trade Center bombing, now just a few days behind us, had our team on high alert even though it wasn't directed at aviation. But a terrorist was a terrorist, a threat a threat, and it was a threat to America and Americans everywhere. So we flew, wishing we had eyes in the backs of our heads too.

As more and more air marshals graduated from training, the FAA gradually increased the number of mission. I watched and felt the increase through the years, but not quite like the surge the program experienced this past year. Now on my last leg, most likely my last mission, I knew I was going to miss being a FAM.

"Maggie, Agent Lopez told me last night during dinner that starting next year the training requirements for marshals' assigned missions was changing significantly."

"In what way?" I asked.

"He said that two days before every mission FAM's will be required to go to D.C. to qualify. Qualify both in PT and firearms. If you fail, you get sent home."

"I guess that's logical," I said, "but it's going to be a logistical nightmare for team scheduling. If someone fails and gets sent home someone will have to be flown in to replace them."

"Yep, and Lopez also told me that more and more law enforcement communities are giving the FAM program a thumbs-up. I mean a thumbs-up with positive recognition for our tactical training skills, our firearms proficiency, and our ability to contribute to the intelligence community. Now that's a real feather in our cap." Randy said.

"It sure is, and I hope I can make a difference in my supervisory position too," I said with a melancholy tone.

"You will Maggie, you will," and Randy walked back to his seat.

CHAPTER 18

Bureaucracy Bound

"I'll call when we get there, I promise."

"You better, I can't believe you're leaving today, and Morgan just got here," Aunt Frances said looking melancholy.

"I know, I know, but at least we got to see her before we go." I said while gazing down at the tiny little girl who had been born just a few hours ago. And it's your birthday tomorrow."

"My best birthday present ever," she said while looking down at her little girl.

Roger was sitting in a chair, his feet up on the bed, watching as she held their new daughter with a very proud look on his face.

Morgan was an absolute cutie-pie. She was a big baby, weighing 9 pounds and ½ ounce. Her tiny hands had long fingers, and her feet had long toes that I hoped would support her throughout her life and guide her happily along.

"She's so beautiful."

Monica and Michael looked on, itchy to do something rather than getting drug around with their mom all day.

"We need to get going," I said, "We've got to get started before the traffic gets really bad."

Roger stood, "Bye-bye," is all he said with his typical smirk and grin. He gave me a pat on the back and a big Texan hug. He tussled both of the kids' hair as we said our farewells.

"I love you guys, and I promise I'll call when I get there," I said leaving her hospital room.

"Seat belts please, you two."

"Watch this Mommy, I can buckle my own belt," Michael proudly said.

"You guys are the best," I said as I backed out of the parking space at Baylor Hospital in North Richland Hills, Texas.

Our blue Dodge Caravan was packed with food, toys, clothes and our dog Sandee. She was a Chow Lab mix that we had adopted 6 months ago.

It was ironic that 18 months after Dave and I divorced, I was moving to Washington, D.C. The phone call I received asking me to apply for a staff position was something I knew eventually need to do. Especially if I ever wanted to advance further in my career. In the FAA D.C. time was an unwritten stepping stone to management positions in the field. It was a difficult decision for me because I was leaving friends and a home in Texas.

Moving to D.C. meant stating all over again; making new friends and finding a place to live. The pay raise to a GS-13 promotion wasn't that significant. The higher cost of living pretty much absorbed any pay raise I was receiving. But I'd been personally recruited for the job so, for me, it was the politically correct thing to do.

So on this hot, humid, typical summer's day, we began our journey that was moving us from Coppell, TX, to Vienna, VA. I was moving on an authorized permanent change of station (PCS) move. I would receive a food allowance, travel expenses, plus mileage for this move. This money would definitely help get us from Texas to Virginia.

"Okay kiddos, we're going to drive 350 miles today. Everyday we're going to stay at a hotel with a pool so we'll be able to swim everyday when we're doing driving. K?"

"K Mommy," Monica said.

"Here we go" I said as I turned onto Interstate 30.

Four days later, after traveling through Texas, Arkansas, Tennessee, and most of the state of Virginia, we arrived safely at the Embassy Suites Hotel just off Chain Bridge Road, in Vienna, Virginia.

"Finally, we made it. Let's go check-in. Bring your backpacks guys and your blankets," I said as I slid open the passenger doors and helped my kids get out of their car seats.

"Stay here Sandee, we'll be right back, Girl." Sandee wagged her tail as if she understood that we were finally going to escape the car for awhile.

Fortunately, since it was still summer, I found a teenager who was recommended to me through St. Mary's Catholic Church. She would watch and play with the kids when I started work the following Monday.

You'll need to figure out other day care when school starts, I thought while waiting for the metro. I barely knew how to use the metro system, much less find the office when I got off the train.

"Let's go, let this adventure begin," I whispered as I stepped on the orange-line train.

The Federal Aviation Headquarters Building was located on the corner of 7th Street S.W. and Independence Boulevard. I'd been there several times, but never from the metro; in the past either by foot from the Holiday Inn Hotel a few blocks away or by cab. Once I got to the building my FAA ID would allow me access, and I knew our offices were on the third floor.

"Hi, I'm Maggie Stewart," I said to the secretary who was located closest to the wide entrance that lead into the Office of Policy and Planning, which is where I was going to work.

"Hi, I'm Laura. Who are you here to see?"

"Bob C."

"Wait right here and I'll go find him for you. They may be in a staff meeting, but let me check."

"Great, thanks."

While waiting, I had time to look around the office space. I had never been in this part of the building before, but without any doubt I knew I was in a government building. It had the look and smell of a government office: the cubicles were gray and bland like most federal buildings, the furniture was drab and completely functional, the carpet looked like the glue down type that came in big squares, and it was very boring. On one of the walls was a picture of the President and Vice-President of the United States. There were windows that faced south, looking out over the train station and several other non-descript looking buildings. People, all with ID's hanging around their necks were coming and going rapidly, as if their lives or careers depended on how quickly they moved through the office space.

Standing near Laura's desk, as people passed, no one greeted me, no one said hello as they sped past as if the papers they had in their hands were of the utmost importance verses greeting another person. *I wonder if this is how it's going to be around here,* I thought.

Laura came back saying, "They are all in a staff meeting. Why don't you go have a cup of coffee and come back in about thirty minutes? They should be done by then."

"Okay, where is the cafeteria again? I've forgotten."

"The Mezzanine level. Take the elevator or stairs, your choice." Laura said as she starting sifting through piles of papers.

At the elevator, I pressed the down button as a man beside me said, "Hey, is that you, Maggie?"

"Hi Marc, how are you? I heard you were working here, where are you?"

"I'm over in Operations, you?"

"Policy and Planning, and it's my first day here,"

My smile faded quickly as Marc told me that he was only here to climb the political ladder. Clearly, he wanted a GS-14 pay grade job over anything else. "Management always wants to promote women, especially women with field experience," Marc said without a smile-and his dark brown eyes boring into me, so contentious, that I wanted to take a few steps backwards to get away from him.

"Okay by me – like I said I just got here. Go for it, Marc. I wish you every success." *Well okay, Maggie, that was fun – NOT.* I decided to take the stairs to escape Marc's negativity. I flew down the stairs two at a time in search of a cup of coffee.

Back upstairs and with a cup of coffee in hand, Bob C. saw me and said "Maggie, it's so great to see you." His thick glasses hung at an angle off his nose. He took my hand and gave me a warm, welcoming, and strong hand-shake.

Just like my Dad, I thought. *He had one heck of a hand-shake too.*

"Before introducing you to everyone on the team, let me show you where your cubicle is. You can put your briefcase down and we'll go from there," Bob said in a hurried voice with his deep New York accent.

I hadn't met Bob before, but we had talked on the phone a few times. He had a fantastic reputation for being fair, intelligent, and funny as hell.

"Here you go, put your things here, and then let me show you around."

"OK," I said putting my briefcase on the seat of the chair.

For the next sixty minutes we walked, talked, and I was introduced to so many people that I couldn't remember everyone's names or what department they worked in.

I think my only saving grace for awhile will be our ID's Badges, I though. *The print is large enough that I can read them from a few feet away.*

"I've enrolled you in a writing class that is specifically geared for new staffers that write policy papers." Bob said. "You'll be starting next Monday, the class is held at the USDA building, directly across the street and its Monday through Friday."

"We need your field experience, and you need our expertise in getting through the bureaucracy. It's a pressure cooker here, but if you like the heat, you'll love this job and this city."

"Okay."

When lunch time came I was on my own. Most employees took thirty minute lunch breaks, even though lunch lasted one hour. This was the unwritten rule in D.C., and no one seemed to mind.

Agent Stanton would be having a fit if he saw this. His wrist watch would be working overtime.

As the days and weeks passed, I fell into a routine. At lunch I decided to walk every day. Most of the federal workers wore tennis shoes to and from their offices, with their work or dress shoes sitting beneath their desks waiting for daylight. I quickly picked up this tradition and changed my shoes throughout the day; once in the morning to come to work, at lunch to walk, and again to go home.

I visited the Smithsonian, the National Memorials and Monuments, the Botanical Gardens, and the Capital since they were all within easy walking distance from the office. The buildings and Mall, as it was called, were full of tourists: old, young, fat, and skinny. They didn't scurry around as quickly as the federal workers did, but the pace was certainly much busier than in Texas. People even talked faster here, you had to be pretty darn quick in meetings to get your two-cents in before management moved on to the next topic.

"I like it here, Aunt Frances." "Riding the metro to and from work is kind of a fun, it's always on time, the view is great, and I'm the last stop on the orange line so I always find a seat. Plus there are tons and tons of free stuff to do in the District. Most of the museums are free."

"How are the kids doing? Where's your ex?"

"Pretty good, I found a little house in Vienna, a block from their school, and within walking distance to the metro station. It's a three bedroom, two bath house, big basement, and I think is has about fifteen oak trees on the property. It's really cute. And it's yellow, one of my favorite colors. Dave lives about twenty minutes away in a condominium complex and sees the kids every other weekend. He's dating again and seems happy."

"How's Roger and Morgan?" I asked

"They are great. Morgan is crawling and getting into everything."

"Gosh. They grow fast that's for sure. I love you, come visit when you can."

"I will. Bye, Girl – love you." Aunt Frances said before hanging up.

As the months passed by, I settled in to my desk job and tried to find a niche in this fast paced city. I discovered that employees in the various departments didn't talk to one another as much as I thought they should. The three divisions, operations, policy, and intelligence, rarely had any meetings together, although top management met every morning at 8:00 A.M. for a staff meeting to brief Associate Administrator for Civil Aviation Security, (ACS-1) on any important events.

Bob C. stopped by every ones cubicle early Monday morning, coffee cup in hand and announced, "All Hands Meeting" at 10:00," he advised each of us.

"K, I'll be there." I said as I continued to work.

"I wonder what we have in store for us now," Joe remarked.

"Guess we'll find out soon enough," I said looking at my watch.
You've got time, Maggie, its only 9 A.M., I thought.

When my head got jammed up with a project I usually slipped on my tennis shoes and went for a walk around the outside of the FAA building. It was fast, close, and a very quick way to get the junk out of my head and move forward.

Well, walking works more times than it doesn't, I said as I skipped down the stairs two at a time.

When I opened the door leading to the ground floor, the door handle slipped out of my grasp and flew open with a force like a winter storm whipping through an alley.

"Whoa, there," said the unsuspecting man. "You almost spilled my coffee."

"I'm so sorry. Are you okay?"

"Yes, I am. I'm Thomas, and you are?"

"Maggie, Maggie Stewart," I said as I reach to shake his hand.

Our touch was magic, sparks flew, and for me the world came to a stand-still. My face felt flush and time seemed to stand still.

"I work in air traffic at National Airport, where do you work?"

"Security, in the Policy and Planning Office, 3rd floor," I said.

"I'm late for my meeting, Maggie but I'll come find you. Yes, I will." he said with a smile crinkling around his lips and with a voice as smooth as silk.

"Well okay – see you. It was nice to meet you Thomas."

Now that was a goof-ball thing to say-nice to meet you-wow, real original, I thought as I headed for the front door.

I made it around the building in record time, zipping past others who had their ID tags hanging around their necks too. *Guess I'm not the only one this morning who needs some fresh air.*

The All Hands meeting started a little late because another meeting in another part of the building lasted longer than expected. Will we waiting we all gathered around outside the conference room, and chatted with Laura, our secretary, and the rest of the team.

"Sorry I'm late," Bob C. said as he started the meeting off. "As you know, it's almost the end of the fiscal year and there's a lot going on around here. I'm happy to announce that we had some funding set aside to give awards this year, unlike last year where we barely had enough funding to meet payroll."

Bob paused and looked around the room.

"With that said, let's give out some awards, shall we?" Bob C. said with a note of fanfare in his voice and mannerisms.

Bill W. received a well deserved cash award for the Hazmat project he had been working on. Nancy and Joyce received awards for the HR manual they were compiling for the organization, and finally, "Gary, I am please to give you this cash award for your excellent work on the AVSEC Security Plan," Bob C. announced.

"Thanks," Gary said with a look of real satisfaction. "Hard work, yes indeed, but it's a beautiful project, if I can say so myself."

For almost six months I had been working with Gary on a joint Aviation Security Manual for Airlines and Airports. The AVSEC Plan outlined the various security requirements that both the airports and airlines needed to follow. The decision had been made to combine the requirements for both regulated entities into one manual; making it easier for both parties to see if any of their procedures would be compatible, overlap or in some way be an asset to one another. Gary and I had spent months talking to the industry, tuning, and refining this plan so it would still meet federal mandates, but would be a viable working document for the aviation industry. It had been exhausting work, but I was very, very proud of what Gary and I had accomplished in considerably a very short time.

Bob C. looked around the room, "Well that's it, thanks guys, and everyone here in this room makes an incredible team. I am very proud to work with such a talented group of individuals."

And it was over!

I can't believe it, that's it? I thought as I walked back to my desk and sat down. *What the hell am I around here, nothing?* I thought while putting on my shoes and coat because I needed a walk in the worst way. I didn't get any recognition for my work and I was half of the team on the project. I was livid!

Feeling the cold wind whipping against my face as I began walking away from the FAA building towards the Capitol, I started to calm down. The cold, blustery fall wind greeting me as a welcomed old friend, seemingly knowing that I needed fresh air.

"I wish I was flying again and back in the field," I said into the cold wind brushing across my face. "But I'm not, so what are you going to do about just getting snubbed, Maggie?"

After walking for nearly an hour I went back upstairs, changed back into my flat, black work shoes, placed my jacket on the coat rack standing just outside of my cubicle and decided I better talk to Bob.

I knocked on Bob's door, "Hi, you got a minute?" I asked.

"Sure, come on in, Maggie. What's on your mind?"

"Bob, I need some feedback on why I didn't receive an award or any recognition today for my portion of the AVSEC plan?"

Bob looked at me in stunned silence.

I went on saying, "I know I'm the newest employee here, and I haven't been here a full year yet, but my contributions were solid, and I've been with the FAA for 8 years now. What happened?"

"Well Maggie, you're still in a significant learning curve here and Gary isn't. He's got a wealth of field experience in aviation and he's really got this policy stuff down. You're still a work in progress."

"Work in progress or not, I still completed my job Bob. Plus half of that AVSEC plan that just got approved is my work. You know that Gary worked on the airline portion of that plan and I worked on the airport sections."

"Agreed," Bob said rubbing his chin, "Let me see what I can do."

"Thanks, that's all I can ask for Bob."

When I got into work the following morning an envelope was sitting on my chair. An inter-office envelope, its bright yellow color in total contrast to the dark gray fabric it was sitting on.

Inside was a single piece of paper describing the superior accomplishments I had achieved while working on the AVSEC Airport Security Plan. The cash award was for the amount of $1,000, the same as Gary's.

Not another word was mentioned about my award.

CHAPTER **19**

The Bojinka Plot

When the doorbell rang I was giddy with excitement. I hadn't been on a date in a very long time. And Thomas was extremely handsome, sexy, funny, and kind.

Monica and Michael were spending the night with their dad and his new wife, Halima. Yes, Dave had remarried and, in a few months time, was moving overseas.

"I'm taking a job in Bangkok, Maggie," Dave had told me one raining evening while we were talking on the phone. "I've given my notice with the FAA and I've accepted a contract position with ICAO. They desperately need inspectors, the pay is fantastic, and I'll be back overseas."

"Really, you quit the FAA?" I said with a touch of sadness for our kids. Once again they wouldn't be seeing their dad very much.

"I already have Maggie. I couldn't get back overseas with the FAA. Halima and I are leaving in two weeks."

Opening the door and seeing Thomas standing on my front pouch, I instantly forgot about Dave and our earlier conversation.

Thomas was smiling with a bouquet of flowers, "Hi, Maggie."

"Hi! Thank you," I said. "Carnations are my favorite. How did you know?"

"Because they are my favorites too."

After giving Thomas the five minute tour of my home, we were on our way to dinner at a local pizzeria in Vienna.

"Would you like me to order for both of us?" Thomas asked when we walked up to the counter, "I don't think you'll be disappointed."

"No, I don't mind at all."

"Okay, we'd like a Sicilian crust, vegetarian, with Alfredo sauce," he told the young girl behind the counter. "Throw every kind of vegetable you can on it, and we'll have two small cokes too."

"You got it," she said as she rang up our order and gave us a number to place on our table.

We found a table by the window, the booths were comfortable, and the place was packed.

"This looks like a real hot spot for a Friday night," I said smiling at Thomas.

"Well, I don't know about that, but I do know the pizza is as about as good as you would get in New York and the price is right."

As I sat looking at Thomas, I saw a man who to me was very handsome. His hairline was receding, he wore thick framed glasses, and his nose looked like it had been broken at least once or twice. He was average built, more on the slender side actually, but you could tell he worked out and cared about his health and appearance. He was neat, clean, and dressed more on the casual side than stylish.

What got to me, what actually soared deep down into my soul was the way he looked at me. Behind those thick framed glasses was a man who listened, who analyzed, watched, and wondered about people and things. He was curious; he wanted to know who I was. He didn't mind that I was divorced, had two kids, was Catholic, and did what I did for a living. In fact, Thomas was a devoted Catholic too. I felt alive just sitting in his presence.

"Where do you go to church, Thomas?"

"Saint James in Falls Church, you," he asked?

"St. Mark, here in Vienna on Vale Road. Church here is a lot different than when I lived in California or even Texas," I said. "I feel a little oppressed here because I'm a woman who is divorced. I recently tried to join the Pastoral Council and was denied because of my divorce. In Texas and especially in California, the church is very welcoming and happy to have people that want to volunteer or help in any capacity. I got over it pretty quickly. I still go to Mass, I think its important not only for me, but especially for Monica and Michael."

"I'm sorry to hear that Maggie. The Catholic Church for me has been a cornerstone in me being able to get through my divorce. My parents were really angry when Kate and I divorced, so for awhile the church was my only friend. I'm glad you're going to Mass."

"Are things better now?"

"Yes, much better. My parents and I are on excellent terms once again."

When the pizza came it was cut in squares, full of veggies, and a thin layer of white sauce on it.

"This is delicious," I said after taking my first bite. I tried really, really hard to not take an over-sized bite for my next taste of this marvelous pizza, but I failed miserable as a few dribbles of Alfredo sauce dripped on my lap.

"Somehow I knew you'd like it Maggie," Thomas said smiling. "And it's pretty good for us too, except for the sauce, but its spread on pretty thin, so we won't have to run too many miles to burn this off."

"Yum, I'll do the miles anytime."

"So who are you, Thomas? How and why did you get into air traffic," I asked between bites.

"I'm originally from Minnesota, but moved to New York after I got out of college. I always wanted to be an air traffic controller, so I started applying as soon as I turned eighteen. I finally landed a job at twenty-one and have been working the boards now for twelve years."

"How long have you been with the FAA?" Thomas asked.

"Seven years now, so I have a little catching up to do."

"I was married, been divorced three years now. I have three kids and they all live in Minnesota. I go up there as much as I can when

I'm off. I do a lot of schedule changes so I can spend time with them. I miss my kids a lot."

And I could see and feel that he did. His facial expressions turned somber, his eating slowed down, and he became melancholy in an instant right before my very eyes.

"I'm sorry, Thomas. I know it must be terrible not being around your kids. When Dave and I split, the kids stayed with me. That's all I wanted or needed. I couldn't believe it was so easy for him to move away."

"Yep, it's a bitch, that's for sure."

"Hey, how about dessert, they have great desserts here." Thomas said as he began turning our somber moods back around.

"I'm stuffed so I think I'll pass on dessert."

"Me too, let's get the check and get out of here. I'm going to need to get you home pretty soon I've got an early shift tomorrow."

At my front door we kissed good night and we promised to go out again next weekend.

"Night my Maggie, sweet dreams and I'll see you next weekend."

Monday morning came way too fast. Nobody wanted to get up. Monica rolled around in her bed, sticking the pillow over her head as if that would help her not to hear the alarm clock.

Michael stomped around the house, with the hardwood floors creaking and crackling beneath his feet. When he finally made it to the bathroom, you could hear the door shut as if he too was in hopes of shutting out the world.

"Well, good morning family," I said while I finished up packing their lunches, "Breakfast will be ready in five minutes."

I let Sandee out to go do her business in the back yard and she even gave me a pitiful look. "Oh, if only I could stay in," she looked up at me with her big eyes.

"Nope, you need to go out, dog," I said, "so scoot."

Dropping the kids off at the before-school day-care center, kissing their cheeks, handing them their lunches, and telling them I loved them as they raced towards the front door: one to get warm, and second to see all of their friends.

"Bye, I love you guys." I said as I stared after them.

I drove the car across the street and parked in the Park and Ride at the Vienna Metro Station. I didn't want to walk in the brisk, cold morning air this morning either.

As I stood on the platform waiting for the train, I smiled and drifted back to my Friday night date with Thomas. I had a wonderful time, and since he called twice over the weekend to say "Hi."

Arriving at the office, the blissfulness joy in my heart immediately dissolved with the news that Bob C. was briefing us on.

"What happened?"

"All we know right now is that two of our agents in Manila, Mary Walsh and Don Harand, reported that a fire erupted in an apartment there, but it wasn't just a fire, it was a fire started from explosives."

He went on to say, "And various documents found in the apartment contained information that outlined a plot to blow up some U.S. aircraft that would be flying into the United States."

The few of us that were already in the office, stood in silence, as Bob continued on, "As we get more information I'll continue to brief you. But rest assured ladies and gentleman, we're about to get very, very busy."

As the days passed, it was discovered that Ramsi Yousef, the same terrorist that had successfully detonated a truck bomb in 1993 at the World Trade Center in New York, was now half way around the world creating another kind of terrorist attack against U.S. citizens. A kind of attack the U.S. Government had never experience before.

"And it appears that Ramsi Yousef has escaped once again," Bob told us just before I headed home for the day.

Riding home on the Metro that day, I wondered if events were going to ramp up again. *It's been pretty quiet in the terrorism arena for the past few years,* I thought to myself. *There's been stuff going on overseas, mostly in Europe, but not here, not in America and not against any U.S. symbols. So what's next?* I wondered.

How anyone can do such things to their fellow human beings, I thought. I knew the answer, was that some people were cold and evil inside, and they had no feeling what-so-ever for others, but still I felt a deep anger inside.

Over the next few weeks, ACS Security Directives went flying across computer screens, fax machines, and into the hands of various airport and airline personnel in response to the liquid explosive threat that was discovered in that tiny apartment fire in Manila. Fortunately for the aviation community, this plot never came to fruition. If it had, the likely-hood that thousands of people would have been killed was very real.

The local fire departments in Manila, those first responders, were the real heroes. They were inside the apartment they recognized the explosive materials and immediately contacted the U.S. CIA for help. Bob C. had told us later that this was a classic case demonstrating that our-meaning the U.S.'s outreach and training-to other countries had really paid off.

"Paid off in that those fire fighters knew what to look for and, when they found suspicious or explosives, they knew who to call," Bob said in our All Hands meeting. "Furthermore, having teams deployed in-country and around Asia when all of this occurred was also a real bonus for FAA Security. A job well done," he said. "The long hours and weeks of hard work have paid off us guys. Thanks."

At the end of another very long day, I got off the metro, walked over to the after school center and picked up Monica and Michael. It was time to go home, let the dog out, and fix something to eat. Thomas was coming by later too, so I had rented a movie for all of us to watch. The kids liked Thomas, well Michael more than Monica, but I think secretly they just didn't want their Mom to date.

"I'm beat guys and I bet you are too. This 6:00 AM to 6:00 PM stuff is for the birds, isn't it?" I said to my kids as we walked home.

"It's okay Mommy," Monica said, "well at least until most of our friends go home at 5:30 PM, but then it gets kind of boring."

"Yep, boring," Michael said. "Then I have to play with her," he said while pointing his finger at his sister.

"Okay, okay you two. Let's get inside and get something to eat. And somebody grab the mail, and let the dog out," I said as I turned the key in the side door the lead into the kitchen.

Michael let the dog out, and Monica got the mail. "Here Mommy, here's the mail."

"Thanks Sweetie, you're the best," I said while giving her a quick hug before she escaped my grasp.

Sifting through the mail, I found the envelope I had been looking for. "Well it's here at last," I said as I tore open the white legal sized envelope. "Let's see what my fate is."

I quickly scanned the letter sent to me by the FAA's Personnel Management Division to ascertain if I had made a selection list for a position I had bid on almost six month ago. A job I had bid on before I met Thomas. If I got the job, it would mean a transfer back to Los Angeles, and a promotion to become the manager for the Los Angeles Civil Aviation Security Field Office.

When the announcement came out, I told my boss, Bob C., that I was going to bid on it. I wanted to get back in the field. I wanted to be closer to my family in California. I'd only been in Washington, D.C., eighteen months, so it was a little premature to bid on another position, but not totally out of the ordinary.

"What I'd like from you, Maggie," Bob told me when I first came to the office, is to spend a year learning how to do this job. Then spend the second year working your ass off doing the job. And then spend the third year figuring out a plan to get out of Washington, D.C. In my opinion, if you stay here more than three years, you never go back to the field." And here it was just a year and a half into the job and I was already trying to find a way to go back to the field. I felt guilt-ridden in a way, but I also knew I needed to get back where I was best suited. And field work, working directly with agents, airline, and airport personnel was where my heart truly was. When I told Bob that I was considering bidding on the position he fully encouraged me to do so. And, I did.

Later that night, after the movie, when the kids were tucked into bed, I told Thomas about the job in L.A. "Work has been so busy with the Bojinka Plot that I totally forgot to tell you, Thomas. Now, what do I do?"

"Let's wait and see, Maggie. These types of decisions don't come easily. I think you know that I'm bidding on a Program Manager's job down at National Airport for the new tower construction there. It's a huge promotion, tons of responsibility, and keeps me here in D.C. So we'll both have decision to make when the time comes."

Here I go again-relationships-but am going to break-up for a job, like Dave did when he left me?

CHAPTER **20**

Sadness In Oklahoma

One of the things I loved most about living in Virginia was fall and spring. In fall, the leaves turn the most beautiful colors and the sky was blue, the air crisp and clean. In spring, it was the same away, expect every plant blooms in celebration of getting through another winter. The bulb tulips, the bougainvillea, and the oak trees were racing to outdo one another by spreading colors far and wide across our neighborhood and beyond.

I loved the big, fat red-breasted Robins, the noisy Blue Jays that squabbled for worms, bugs, and for the small pieces of bread that Monica and Michael threw out in the back yard. Even Sandee got in the game, barking and chasing every animal in sight. It was a glorious time of year to be living near Washington, D.C.

My telephonic interview had gone well for the manager's position in L.A. My only big competition, I felt, was Agent Lee Stanton. He was a personal hero of mine, and I felt bad competing against him, but sometimes you needed to do what was best for your career and family.

"Good luck, Maggie," Stanton said when I had called him earlier in the week to let him know that I had applied.

The candidates weren't supposed to know who we were competing against, but the rumor mill was very much alive and well in ACS.

It was a juicy bit of information, a scandal, or something that was supposed to be kept on the QT, so-to-speak, but it always surfaced. Somehow word always leaked out, as was in this case.

"You too Stanton, when's your interview?" I asked.

"Tomorrow at 11:00 A.M., how about yours?"

"Tomorrow, but at 2:00 PM., but mine's telephonic"

"Sounds good – good luck" and we both hung up.

Before the interview got started Agent Bones said, "Hello Maggie, it's been a long time since we've spoken to one another hasn't it?

"Morning," I said.

"I've got you on speaker phone so I can take notes."

Agent Bones was the Division Manager for the Western-Pacific Region now, but the last time we met was in Rome, Italy. He was a supervisor at the office there. Normally, when FAMS were in countries where there was an FAA Security Office, we'd stop by. Our visit was to ascertain if there was any information that might be useful for the team. And second it was a courtesy to visit when possible.

Agent Bones was available to see us; in fact, he insisted that we all walk to his favorite pizzeria for lunch. We walked those few blocks to a small pizzeria with outdoor seating, and proceeded to dine on the most delicious thin-crusted pizza I had ever had. I can still recall the vivid colors of various vegetables adorning it, as the vivid colors of people's clothing earlier had dotted the street surrounding us. We all ate with gusto, enjoying the meal not only for its flavor, but for its beauty.

"Pizza, I remember you and the pizza," I said.

"Yes," he said with a chuckle. "I miss Rome, but I really miss the food."

My interview lasted about thirty minutes. We talked about the staffing for the office, airports, airlines, management styles, even the economy. It was a fast-paced interview peppered with lots of questions. I knew the geographical area for the LAX CASFO very well. And I wasn't afraid of the expensive housing market their so I was confident my knowledge and the answers I gave demonstrated that I would make a great CASFO Manger.

When I hung up the phone I thought, *well that went pretty well, so we'll see what happens next. But in the meantime I need to get back to work here.*

After months of writing Security Directives and Emergency Amendments to enhance the security procedures for U.S. Air Carriers operating in and out of the United States, we were all getting used to the long hours at the office. The pace was maddening and the work hours grueling, but they paled in comparison to what the agents in Asia were doing. Because of the time difference, the agents there were getting calls at all hours of the night, and they were conducting inspections during the day.

Bob C. looked fatigued as well, and I knew the reason why: he was the only policy representative for the daily staff meetings and various telecoms that were taking place because of the Bojinka Plot.

"Hey, Bob, nice surprise," I said, "I never see you on the metro, and I have to say, you look worn out."

"Yes, I'm exhausted," he said to me as we walked off the metro together after accidently running into one another. "But the agents in Asia are really taking the brunt of things. Those guys work at the airport all day, make sure the SDs and EAs we send them are implemented, then they go back to the hotel to write their daily trip reports, and then they have to decide to either stay up the rest of the night or get a few precious hours of sleep before their 3:00 A.M. telecom!"

"Yikes, that's crazy. I forgot about the dramatic time zone difference for them," I said.

"Crazy in the sense that I think we should be staying up late here and letting the agents that are deployed do their jobs and then get some sleep. They are our eyes and ears, and we really need them to be alert. I worry about them sometimes."

"I've heard Mary Walsh in Manila is one kick-ass, incredible agent."

"You better believe it," Bob C. said. She's absolutely the best there is. The FAA was so fortunate that she was in-country when the shit hit the fan over there. And the extraordinary thing is that we didn't used to deploy many agents to Asia."

"Why haven't we?" I curiously asked, "I don't know very much about our international work. I was a FAM and I've only done a few international assessments," I said to Bob.

"Do you remember Philippines Flight 434 back in December last year?"

"Vaguely, a bomb under a seat killed one guy," I responded.

"That's the one," Bob said. "It was the work of Ramis Yousef. In fact, he placed the bomb on the flight. It originated out of Manila with a stop in Cebu and then it was scheduled to fly on to Narita. Well, lucky for that flight and those passengers, Yousef placed the bomb in the wrong position-sideways versus up and down-so when the bomb went off it blew up and down, not side to side. It was hidden where a life vest was supposed to be so there was a buffer. Consequently, only one passenger was killed, the poor Japanese Businessman in Seat 26K."

"Okay, I remember now, and we deployed agents throughout Asia because of it to ensure the airlines follow all the new security procedures we implemented."

"Fortunately, for us the front office recognized the immediate need to deploy agents overseas, and I have to admit it saved us in Manila." Bob said.

"So, when do you think the telecoms will slow down?" I asked.

"Not for awhile I suspect, Maggie, not for awhile."

On Monday, April 19, 1995, in Oklahoma City, Oklahoma, the evil winds of terrorism shifted again, sadly back onto U.S. soil. This time it struck very close to our hearts; here in the heartland of America.

Around 10:30 A.M., Bob yelled, "Okay team, get here now."

I got up from my chair and quickly walked over to the conference room. *Bob never yells, what's happened?* I wondered.

Watching the TV we soon saw why Bob yelled. A special news alert banner was flashing across the television and CNN was reporting that there had been a massive explosion at the Alfred P. Murrah Federal building, in Oklahoma City, Oklahoma.

The TV cameras zoomed in on a building that clearly looked like a bomb had gone off. The north side of the nine-story building was a shattered mess of debris. The news reporter said it looks as if one third of the building had been destroyed.

"Shit, shit, shit," a fellow colleague uttered in disbelief and disgust.

The TV showed emergency response teams, police, fire, federal, and citizens all descending on the building in an effort to help the wounded, injured, and cover the dead. Men, women, and children were filmed walking around in a daze.

Later that week, during our weekly Friday meeting, Bob C. said, "I know you all read the papers and watch the news, but it was reported this morning that without a doubt people perished, and many, many more were injured. And yes, many of them are still hospitalized. The destruction to surrounding buildings was reported to be massive."

"We're going to need to pitch in and help Dave, the aviation facilities office director and his team with writing additional security measures for our federal buildings around the country. The front office has authorized field agents to come in and work here for 30 day details. Plus we have unlimited overtime authorization to assist in any way possible. So who's in?" he asked.

Everyone raised their hands.

"Good, it looks like we're all in this together then."

"Timothy McVeigh has been arrested along with Terry Nichols. They have both been charged. What we know so far about McVeigh is that he's an American militia movement sympathizer and a Gulf War vet. He is the one that detonated the explosive-filled Ryder rental truck."

"This is going to be a huge investigation by the FBI, so we'll see how, when, and if we can assist them. In the meantime here is a sensitive document that I want each of you to read now while we're in this room. It's time to protect our home, ladies and gentlemen."

"On a positive note, the news reported this morning that over 12,000 people have participated in some type of relief and rescue efforts. And Americans are sending in donations for the families through the American Red Cross or United Way," I said. "A sad, sad event, but we're America; we're going to help our own."

After walking into our staff meeting on Friday, the 5th of May, I sat down beside Laura, our division secretary and I looked around the room at the team. By the look on everyone's face, you could see the exhaustion in their eyes. The mental strain of working long hours, eating fast-food, little to no sleep was beginning to show.

"Okay, I'm going to make this quick and then I'm giving everyone an hour of paid administrative leave," Bob said.

I smiled, "You mean the 59 minute rule, Bob?" I asked.

"That would be the one. It's time for a break. But first, let me tell you that the rescue and recovery efforts have concluded and all but three bodies have been recovered. Sadly, 165 people were killed, 680 were injured, and the total buildings damaged or destroyed was around 324. And the estimated cost so far is around $652 million dollars worth of damage!"

"Whoa," Laura said.

"So starting Monday, I'll ask again for volunteers to finish helping Dave and his team put the final touches on the new Facilities Security Manual that we want organizational approval on ASAP. We're close, but we need a few more eyes and ears. "

Without Bob having to ask, everyone raised their hand.

"I knew it, I just knew it. Now, get out of here and go home, hug your families, and pray that we never have to do this again."

As I turned the corner, seeing my little yellow house on Myers Circle I smiled because Thomas' car was parked in front of the house.

Just as I walked up to the side door to go in the house, Thomas was going out the front door with a duffle bag.

"Hey, hi, what are you doing here?" I said walking up to him and expecting to get a kiss. But, in return, I got a look mixed with sadness and guilt.

"Hiya, Maggie, I wasn't expecting you."

"I can see that, Thomas, what are you doing? Leaving me?"

He tossed his duffle bag onto the back seat of his car and walking up to me, he said, "Let's sit down, Maggie."

"I know you want to move to L.A., you want to go home, but I have decided I'm going to stay here. I got my job offer today as the Program Manager for the new tower project at National. It's what I want to do, Maggie. Plus, I'm closer to my kids here than if I moved to L.A."

"But Thomas, I haven't even been offered a position yet. What if I don't get it? Everything about us works-how-why has that changed? Can't we work this out?" I said as tears began forming in my eyes.

"It's just changed. You want to go back to California and I want to stay here. That fact for us won't change. I have to do what's best for me, a promotion, a serious job that I really want to do, and I'm closer to my kids."

"I know you want to stay here. I know I want to go back to California for the same reason you want to stay here; a promotion, a serious job that I really want to do, and I'm closer to my family."

Thomas listened as I kept talking, "I know I've been working some incredibly long hours lately and I haven't seen you as much as I've wanted to. That's my fault. I know we both had really serious decisions to make about our jobs, but I thought we'd talk more about this Thomas. I didn't think I'd come home to see you packing."

Leaning over and hugging me, he said, "I know. I'm sorry Maggie, but I have to go."

I saw the pain in his eyes as I watched him go, the car tail lights fading as he turned the corner.

"Well, another relationship down the drain for a career." I said as I sat on the steps and cried.

CHAPTER **21**

Another Madman Strikes

After last Friday's sudden departure of my boyfriend, Thomas and then my basement flooding, I was in a really foul mood.

The plumber that arrived late Sunday night with dollar signs in his eyes told me that my sump pump had stopped and that's why there was water in the basement.

"What the heck is a sump pump?" I asked.

"Oh, you're not from around here, are you?"

"Do I sound like I am?" I said though clenched teeth.

"Hey, Mom, I'm hungry." Monica said calling down from the top of the stairs.

"Hungry? You're supposed to be in bed, young lady, now scoot." I hollered.

"Please, Mom, I'm really hungry."

"Oh, good grief, then grab a banana Monica. I'll be right up."

I looked at the plumber and said, "Well, now that you've determined it's the sump pump, can you fix it?"

"I can and will, but it will cost you $300 dollars, for the part and the weekend service call." He replied.

"I don't think I have much choice, unless I want the rest of my books floating around down here. Or maybe I should just turn the basement into an indoor swimming pool. I could charge an entry fee and probably make some money. What do you think? Good idea?"

"Well, no ma'am, that isn't a very good idea," he replied not sure if I was kidding him or not.

"All right then, I'll get my checkbook and you get a sump pump. We'll trade, a check for a pump. Is that a deal or what?"

"That's a deal, and I'll get right on it," he said sliding past me faster than I imagined his fat, out-of-shape body could do.

"Yikes, I need a glass of wine," I thought, *"But right now I'm going to check on my kids!"*

Monica was back in bed with her eyes wide-open. "Oh, you're going to be in great shape for tomorrow, aren't you Kiddo," I said as I rubbed her head.

"I can always miss a day of school, Mom."

"Not a chance, I can't miss work, and you guys can't miss school."

"Darn."

"Darn tooting and good night, Honey, I'll see you in the morning."

"Love you," I said as I partially closed her bedroom door.

I checked on Michael and he was asleep – out like a light. "Sleep well little guy." I tipped toed over and kissed him on top of the head too.

After paying the plumber I poured myself a full glass of wine and sat down at the kitchen table. "I know I'm going to pay for this later, but right now, I just want wine." I said out loud.

"It's okay, I'm not talking to myself, I'm talking to the dog." and I peered down at Sandee who was sound asleep beside the wall heater in the living room.

"Well, maybe I am talking to myself."

I thought how crazy the past few months had been. If it hadn't been for my neighbor, Rose, I would have never gotten through the trials and tribulations of work and then Thomas.

Rose watched the kids for me if I was going to pick the kids up later than 6 P.M. from the after school program. I was hardly ever that late, but having a back-up when needed was a lifesaver.

Thomas was gone, not a phone call since he left, not a word, it's as if our relationship had never existed. Staring into my wine glass, I said, "I am a complete failure when it comes to a relationship, that's for sure."

"Okay off to bed with you," I said out loud. I put my empty wine glass on the kitchen counter, looked out into the dark void of the back yard, switched off the light, and headed to bed.

"Amazing," I said, "you actually got up for work, you didn't call in sick. Way to go, Maggie."

"Come on guys we'll all be late, I can't miss my Metro." I hollered out again. "Let's get a move on."

And with stomping feet-all three of us stomping our feet-we shut the door behind us and headed off into the world. "It's a fine day, guys," I said as we walked to McClain Elementary School.

"I want a croissant today," I said as I stepped off the Metro at L'Enfant Plaza Metro Station. "I'll think I'll splurge and have a cup of coffee too."

While waiting, I watched the hundreds of people scurrying along the open air corridor that led to the metro station and various office buildings. Washington, D.C., was political, fast-paced, challenging, interesting, and a tad bit magical. "I never get bored here, that's for sure," I said while grabbing my coffee, my brown-bagged croissant, and a "thanks, keep the change."

As I climbed the worn, dirty, gray stairs up to the third floor, I was carefully balancing my coffee in one hand and my briefcase in the other. I had stuffed my croissant in the top of my briefcase, not really caring if it got smashed. *I just care how it tastes.* I said in anticipation of biting into the rich, buttery roll.

I sat down in my chair, bent over, untied my shoes laces, and took off my tennis shoes. I grabbed the now dull, black flat dress shoes and put them on. *My former drill sergeant in the Navy would be embarrassed to see my shoes in this condition*, I thought. I powered up my computer and glanced at my telephone to see if the message light was blinking. It was. I picked up the receiver the phone emitted a beeping sound that notified me that I had a message.

While sipping my coffee, I dial the message number to retrieve the voicemail of whoever called me between Friday afternoon and Monday morning. I was glad to hear Mr. Bones, the Division Manager from Los Angeles, leaving me a message to please call him at my earliest convenience.

I can't call him now, its 4:00 AM in California. I'll just have to wait a few hours, but it's a really good sign! "Guess I'll just have to get some work done instead," I said out loud.

I was working on a white paper that outlined the impact if the United States should add any additional items to the current embargo on Iran. That embargo had been placed since March. I was directed to write what the pros and cons would be if aviation companies were banned from selling aircraft and repair parts to Iranian Airlines. Executive Order (EO) 12957 placed heavy restrictions on oil products and now several months later President Clinton wanted information regarding aviation restrictions.

The first EO had been signed shortly after the exiled Shaw of Iran was permitted to enter the United States, and in protest the U.S. Embassy in Iran was seized and U.S. Citizens had been taken hostage.

Drafting any high-level document was stressful enough, in my opinion, but the draft I was staring at had three pros, those being: 1. We would potentially be creating an unsafe aircraft fleet by not providing the necessary parts to maintain their aircrafts; 2. This action would then possibly jeopardize the lives of anyone that flew on any Iranian Airline; 3. U.S. business would be impacted here in the U.S., e.g. Boeing. I could only think of two cons and those were: 1. human rights issue, since Iran had already jeopardized human lives through their actions against the U.S. Embassy, and we should not condone that type of activity; and 2. under no circumstances should we give into the political views or demands of terrorists.

There has to be another solution.

I was also advised that the International Civil Aviation Organization (ICAO) had been putting a great deal of political pressure on the United States stating that if the U.S. imposed such an aviation sanction that it would endanger aviation safety in that part of the world, which was contrary to Article 44 of the Chicago Convention.

As I continued to stare at my half-page draft, I could feel a headache beginning to cut across my forehead. *Whew, you've got your hands full on this, Maggie. I know airports, airplanes, and security pretty darn well, but...* the ringing of the telephone interrupted my thoughts.

"Good morning, Office of Policy and Planning, Maggie Stewart," I said answering the phone.

"Maggie, it's Mr. Bones from Los Angeles. How are you?"

"Great, thank you. I got your voicemail, but I was going to wait a few hours to call you, since it's still pretty early out there."

"I've got a couple of early meetings today, so I decided to call you while I had a minute," He said. "So are you ready to come and work for me?"

"You bet I am," I said. "I am ready sir."

"Good to hear because I've selected you for the manager's position here. You had some tough competition, but you're a good fit for this office and I am looking forward to bringing you onboard."

"Thank you so, so much! I am really looking forward to the opportunity as well. And I'm coming home; I'll be near my family and friends again."

"I'm working on a July 16th pick-up date, so I'll keep you posted. I talked to Bob on Friday so he is already aware that we are stealing you away and back to the Western-Pacific Region."

"Gosh, thanks so much." I said.

"Bye for now, Maggie. My secretary Donna will call you as things progress." Mr. Bones said.

Before hanging up the phone, out of the corner of my eye, I saw Bob standing at the opening to my cubicle. *He's smiling, so that's a good sign,* I thought.

"I guess you heard the good news, Maggie?" Bob said.

Suddenly, a few heads popped up from their cubicles and said in unison, "What good news? What?"

"Well go on, tell them," Bob urged.

"I got picked up as the CASFO Manager at LAX." I jubilantly said.

"Hey! Way to go, Maggie. Drinks are on you after work," the team chanted while clapping their hands together.

With all the commotion, more heads popped up above their cubicles and the party size increased.

The small gathering at the French Bistro across the street from the office was the perfect location to end the day. Happy hour was in full swing and the EL'Faunt Metro Station was several floors beneath us underground. So we could toast a few spirits and not have to drive home.

"Okay everyone, the first round is on me, and then you're on your own. I've got kids that will need to see their mom in about an hour, plus I don't have my pay raise yet," I said smiling at my fellow co-workers.

"Works for us," Bob said as lightly held the hand of his beautiful girlfriend, Sandra.

"We don't know what you see in him, Sandra," Gary yelled out.

She said as she looked dreamily at Bob. "He's my guy, and I love him so."

"Whoa, your blushing, Bob," I said.

"Run, Maggie, run, or you'll be late," I yelled out loud as I jay-walked across Nutley Street. The after school program was great, but if you were late you were charged one dollar for every minute you were late. "I can't afford the late charge, so run, girl, run."

I made it at the stroke of 6:00 P.M., grabbed my tired and hungry kids and we walked home to see what we could stir up for dinner.

While we ate spaghetti and toast, I said, "Hey, guess what guys?"

"What Mommy?" Monica said between bites.

"I got a promotion today, and in July, in about a month from now, we're going to move to California."

They both looked at me and were very, very quiet. "How are we going to see our friends, Mommy? I don't want to move away from Loren." Monica said.

"What about football?" Mike said.

"There will be friends, football, and family in California," I said. "It will be okay, trust me you guys, it will be okay."

"And the beach, remember the beach?" I quickly added in hopes that it would cheer them up.

It didn't cheer them up, not a bit, no sir, not one bit.

When school got out for the summer, the only thing that changed for the kids was they went to a summer program all day. Days full of fun activities, friends, and field trips. They seemed to be having a great time. At least they were tired and full of dirt by day's end. Tired and dirty was always a good measuring stick in my book.

The house went up for sale and sold quickly, a little below what I had originally hoped for, but due to a recent Mobile Oil lay off in the D.C. area, I couldn't complain.

At 9:00 P.M. on my second to last day working in Washington, D.C., the house phone rang.

"Hello?"

"Maggie, this is Bob. You need to come into the office ASAP." He said in a very urgent voice.

"Oh, come on Bob. You're kidding me right? My last day in D.C. is tomorrow, so you're kidding me – right?"

"No, we have an emergency directive that needs to go out to-night. I need your help. Come into the office immediately."

"No kidding, right?"

"No kidding, Maggie. This is the real deal. Get here as soon as you can."

Monica and Mike were already in bed, boxes, and bags were all over the house. Sandee looked up at me with sleepy eyes; I suspect she was hoping I wasn't going to send her outside at this time of night.

"Rose, this is Maggie, next door. There's an emergency at work and I have to go in immediately," I said to my neighbor.

"Go, go, I'll be right over," she said.

"You are a life-saver," I said, "I'll never be able to thank you enough."

I backed my van out of the driveway at 9:30 P.M., heading towards the District. I knew the drive would take about twenty minutes at this time of night. After normal business hours federal employees, with proper identification could park in the FAA building, so I didn't need to worry about meter parking or find a garage that was open late.

When I got to the office it was abuzz with people, noise, and every kind of activity you could imagine. Fax machines were cranking away, you could hear nails clicking on keyboards and telephones were ringing on desks, conference tables, and private offices. If I wasn't the last one in the office, I was close to the last one.

"What's happening?" I asked as I walked towards the conference room.

"The Unabomber struck again," Gary, one of the staffers, said.

I immediately stood taller, feeling my eyes narrowing and my ears engaging to collect any additional information – I already knew it was going to be a long night.

The Unabomber was a familiar name to us in security. The FBI used the title "UNABOM" for University and Airline Bomber. Since May 1978, there had been sixteen bombs targeted against universities and airlines, three people had been killed so far, and twenty-three had been injured. The latest death had occurred in April of this year in Sacramento, CA.

Bob C. hollered, "Okay, I think everyone is here. Let's jam into the conference room and let me bring everyone up to date."

"Listen up, the FBI has asked that the Department of Transportation and the United States Postal Service (USPS) work together to come up with security measures to get a handle on and stop packages with explosives in them from getting mailed or flown to unsuspecting people and having them blow up on them."

Bob continued on, "I know you've all heard about the last incident in California where a timber industry lobbyist was killed from a package he received in the mail."

"You guys are the team, the team consisting of: the Hazmat security, cargo security, airline security, airport security, two USPS staffers, and a runner. We are going to write, rewrite, and write until we come up with acceptable policies and procedures to thwart the Unabomber. Bill Wilkening is the team lead for this project. He's the best there is. Understood? Are there any questions?"

"And Maggie, I have a special request, not only are you going to be the airport security specialist, I need you to be the typist too! You're the fastest and we need to get this done, NOW!"

I nodded, "Okay, I'll warm up these fingers," I said which cracking a few.

"You're weird!" Gary said.

"Thank you, thank you very much," I said with the best Elvis impersonation I could muster.

As the night wore on, we wrote, re-wrote, and wrote more. We stuffed papers into the burn box for shredding later, and worked till our fingers got so stiff we could hardly type. Our brains became so tired we could hardly think.

But, by dawn, we had excellent draft document that airport, airlines, and the postal service could use to prevent packages with explosives getting on any aircraft or into U.S. mail box.

"Great job, everyone. Now, we've got some solid paper to show the front office this morning." Bob said.

Bob patted me on the shoulder, "God, I knew you typed fast, but I didn't know you typed that fast, Maggie. We got it done, we all put our heads together and our talents and we got it done."

"Yes, we did Bob, yes we did. And Bill Wilkening from Hazmat, what a genius that guys is. I hope I can work with him again someday." I said.

"He's a talented and feisty guy. He can make the subject of Hazmat totally interesting. We are lucky to have him here with the FAA and not with Federal Highways, where the Hazmat Regulations are written."

"Go home, Maggie. Get some breakfast, and we'll see you later."

"Okay, I need to move my car out of the garage anyway. If I don't, whoever's space I'm in won't be very happy."

Walking down to my car, I felt a sense of pride that I hadn't felt in a long time. Politics, fast-paced environments, and stress sometimes aren't always a great combination, but today, I once again saw dedication, strength, and the will to fight to keep our country safe.

"I love this job. I love this job!" I said as I unlocked my car door.

When I got home, I hugged Rose, and said, "You are a life saver."

The moving van was coming at 3:00 P.M. to pack up the house, and Rose kindly offered us to stay at her house versus getting a hotel for the night. "I'll tell you more about what happened when I see you later."

I cooked the kids breakfast, got them off to day camp, showered, changed, and went back to the office. I drove in again, parking about three blocks from the office and walked.

"Just a few more hours, Maggie, let's see what else needs to be done," I said as I walked into the office.

"Surprise," everyone shouted when walked into the office.

"You didn't think you were getting away without a party, did you?" Bob asked.

"You guys are wonderful!"

"Here's your card, and please cut the cake so we can have some breakfast," Gary said with a laugh.

"You got it. Gosh, thanks, guys."

The following morning, with kisses and hugs, we bid Rose good-bye and promised to write when we got to California. "Drive safe," she said.

With Monica and Michael safely buckled in, and Sandee sitting beside Michael, I jumped in the driver's seat, buckled my seat-belt, looked in the rear-view mirror, and began backing out of the driveway for the long, long awaited journey to California.

I realized how much I had learned in the past few years: about myself, about the agency, about the importance of our jobs. I watched dedicate people every single day walk into the headquarters building never fully knowing what to expect with each given day. The scope of their workload depended on what the terrorist were planning, but every day they came into work prepared.

The Office of Policy and Planning was a cornerstone to the fields' operational strategies. I knew that now. The policies and regulations we wrote in D.C. helped protect lives. Now I was going back to the field to help implement them.

No matter what office we worked in, or position we held, we've all been hired to defend.

Acknowledgments

To my editor Sierra Meffan-Jahoda

To the staff at Outskirts Press, Denver, Colorado

To my children Monica Lyons, Michael Noaker, and their families

To my sister Sylvia Dietsch, my brother Timothy Sawyer, and their families

To my writing class instructor, Ruth Herbert, and my fellow students

To my dear friends and former colleagues at the FAA

Thank you from the bottom of my heart.